The Breakdown
of Higher Education

The Breakdown
of Higher Education

How It Happened, the Damage It Does,
and What Can Be Done

John M. Ellis

BOOKS

New York • London

First American edition published in 2020 by Encounter Books,
an activity of Encounter for Culture and Education, Inc.,
a nonprofit, tax-exempt corporation.
Encounter Books website address: www.encounterbooks.com

Manufactured in the United States and printed on
acid-free paper. The paper used in this publication meets
the minimum requirements of ANSI/NISO Z39.48–1992
(R 1997) (*Permanence of Paper*).

FIRST AMERICAN EDITION

LIBRARY OF CONGRESS CATALOGING-IN-PUBLICATION DATA

Names: Ellis, John M. (John Martin), 1936– author.
Title: The breakdown of higher education: how it happened,
the damage it does, and what can be done / by John M. Ellis.
Description: First American edition. | New York: Encounter Books, 2020.
Includes bibliographical references and index.
Identifiers: LCCN 2019043565 (print) | LCCN 2019043566 (ebook)
ISBN 9781641770880 (cloth) | ISBN 9781641770897 (ebook)
Subjects: LCSH: Education, Higher—United States. | Education,
Higher—Political aspects—United States.
Classification: LCC LA227.4. E55 2020 (print) | LCC LA227.4 (ebook)
DDC 378.73—dc23
LC record available at https://lccn.loc.gov/2019043565
LC ebook record available at https://lccn.loc.gov/2019043566

CONTENTS

PREFACE

In the years immediately following the Second World War, America's colleges and universities enjoyed the almost unlimited confidence of the American people. Enrollments soared, and many new campuses were built across the country. That confidence has been draining away as stories of education corrupted by radical politics have grown increasingly common, and politically correct foolishness has brought ridicule upon one campus after another. In the last few years, however, the erosion of public trust in higher education has accelerated. The public has seen more and more instances of speakers who challenge any aspect of radical leftist orthodoxy being shouted down and silenced on campuses. The rot that has been growing for many decades appears to have reached a point of no repair.

It is some thirty years since we began to see books warning of the destructive direction that higher education was taking. Allan Bloom's *The Closing of the American Mind: How Higher Education Has Failed Democracy and Impoverished the Souls of Today's Students* appeared in 1987. Roger Kimball's *Tenured Radicals: How Politics Has Corrupted Our Higher Education* came out in 1990. Dinesh D'Souza's *Illiberal Education: The Politics of Race and Sex on Campus* was published in 1991. My own book *Against Deconstruction* (1989) looked at one particular feature of the intellectual decay that was just beginning, one that had become entrenched on college campuses in spite of its complete incoherence.

In retrospect, it now appears to me that we were all writing to diagnose a developing problem and to persuade academic colleagues that the direction in which they were taking higher education would be disastrous. Radical politics was a rising force on the campuses, and we were trying to draw attention to the dangers in what was happening while there was still some chance of arresting it. But it's now clear that we failed to stop the slide, because the political radicals on campus never had any interest in what we had to say. Their purposes were not ours. We were interested in the quality of higher education, but what they cared about was getting control of the campuses so that they could use them to promote their political ideology, one so unpopular with the general public that it could not have been advanced in any other way. We got to this point not because they didn't foresee the grim results of what they were doing—the virtual destruction of higher education as we have known it—but because they did. They were of course assisted by other factors that are always present in human life: the complacency of those many people who are always prone to think alarms overwrought, and the reluctance of others to allow themselves to seem allied with conservatives by opposing a leftist program, however extreme it might be.

And so there is no point in yet another book that diagnoses a growing problem and warns of its consequences. It's too late for warnings about what may happen because it has already happened: the corruption of the campuses by radical politics is now well advanced. Accordingly, this book is of a different kind. Its purpose is threefold: first, to explain exactly what happened and what made it possible; next, to describe the frightening extent of the damage that has been done to all levels of education, including K–12, as well as the equally serious damage that is now being done to our society as a result; and finally, to consider what can be done about this educational and societal catastrophe.

Unlike those books of thirty years ago, this one is not addressed to professors, because they are now the locus of the problem. Instead, it is addressed to people outside the academy who still have the good sense they were born with—something no longer common on college campuses—and who want the universities to provide what they formerly did: a fine education for themselves and their children, well-researched and carefully presented commentary on the major issues of the day, and valuable social, scientific, and technological research. This book is for people who know well enough already that the considerable sums of money they contribute to higher education both through their taxes and through tuition payments are much more dubious investments than they once were—and who want to understand how this happened and what can be done about it.

CHAPTER 1

What Do Those Near-Riots Tell Us about the State of Higher Education?

The public's already declining confidence in academia has recently been jolted by a series of violent campus events, some of which
could legitimately be called riots. Student mobs have prevented invited
guests from speaking on campuses such as UC Berkeley, UCLA, and
Middlebury College. On other campuses, faculty members have been
subjected to harassment campaigns for expressing opinions contrary
to the reigning orthodoxy. The denial of free speech in campus public
spaces has become widely known, but while it is certainly an important
issue, it doesn't get to the heart of what has been happening to our campuses. In this chapter I want to go deeper into these events to examine
what they really tell us about the state of higher education.

The assault on free expression in the public sphere is best regarded
as a relatively superficial symptom of much larger problems that need
to be understood and dealt with before we will ever be able to restore
genuine respect for freedom of speech on the campuses. If tomorrow
every campus in the nation were to start ensuring that visiting speakers
are never again shouted down, the underlying sickness of higher education would remain untouched. We cannot understand the nature of the
sickness until we ask: *Why* is free speech constantly under threat on the
campuses? Why do shout-downs and near-riots now occur with such
regularity? These questions lead to the broader subject of how higher
education has been so thoroughly corrupted and diverted from its real
purpose.

This nation's major universities have always had much prestige, which is another way of saying that the public stood in awe of them. A Harvard University degree always transferred some of that institution's prestige to the student who earned it, but during the last three decades the prestige of colleges and universities has been declining. People have become increasingly skeptical about them—all of them, not just the minor ones. A steady drip of stories about grade inflation, political correctness, identity politics, political advocacy in the classroom, trivialization of the curriculum, kangaroo courts, a dearth of classes that educate for citizenship—and much more besides—has diminished the respect that universities enjoy. Now the much-publicized shouting down of visiting speakers has dramatically accelerated the decay in the standing of academia.

Harassment of visiting speakers on campus is not really new in itself: for many years now, hecklers have been disrupting lectures by conservative guests. What has changed is that the disrupters' behavior has become more determined, more spiteful, and more indiscriminate. Only recently have we seen a violent mob absolutely set on preventing a scheduled lecture from taking place, and willing to use physical threats and assault to make sure of that.

The threat of violence is of course not just about canceling a particular speech. The aim is to intimidate and discourage future speakers too, so that certain kinds of ideas will never be heard on campus. And these threats have been quite successful: campus administrations have often used the likelihood of violence as a reason for canceling a lecture. In so doing, they have been willing to reward mobs who threaten violence by giving them what they want preemptively. It's easy to understand why violent mob action would be effective in causing vulnerable small-business owners to capitulate, but much harder to understand why university presidents would cave to extortion by their own faculty and students.

The series of events that have riveted the public's attention began on February 1, 2017, with a riot on the Berkeley campus of the University of California on the occasion of a planned speech by Milo Yiannopoulos, a gay conservative. Fires were set and buildings damaged ahead of the planned talk, which was then canceled. While that event was fresh in everyone's mind, another at Middlebury College on March 2 raised public awareness of politically inspired violence on campus still more: the distinguished sociologist Charles Murray and a Middlebury College professor, Alison Stanger, were physically attacked as they left the lecture hall at the end of Murray's talk, which protesters had tried unsuccessfully to stop by making as much noise outside the building as they could. Stanger was injured and had to be hospitalized. The mob didn't stop there: they pursued Murray after he had left campus to go to a dinner with friends. Then, on April 5, Heather Mac Donald was shouted down at UCLA after she had finished only half of her planned talk, and the next day her talk at Claremont McKenna College was effectively canceled by another menacing crowd. In May, Evergreen State College descended into complete chaos after a group of black students had announced that whites should all leave campus for a day, and Professor Bret Weinstein objected to this attempt to discriminate by race. Both students and faculty harassed him so viciously that he and his wife were in effect hounded into retiring from their faculty positions.

By this time, the public was paying attention to campus thuggery as never before, and anxiety about it was growing. In the past, heightened public attention had often been enough to make campus radicals stop what they were doing, but now it was different: these lamentable events actually became more and more frequent. Later that year, Stanley Kurtz summarized what happened next:

> The spring semester of 2017 will long be known for popularizing this fearsome technique of speech suppression. Remarkably, however, as we approach the halfway mark of the Fall 2017 semester, the rate of shout-downs is now nearly quadruple that of last spring. I count 19 shout-downs so far this year. At the current rate, that would make for 38 fall-semester shout-downs. This would nearly quadruple the 10 shout-downs of last spring, a semester already infamous for speaker disruptions.[1]

What then do these events say about the overall health of college campuses? The most important issue that emerges in every one of them is the way in which the academy now deals with political ideas. The traditional academy specialized in analyzing them: it examined the pros and cons, the strengths and weaknesses of any idea, and looked into what the historical record showed of the opportunities and dangers it held. But what these recent campus episodes demonstrate is that advocacy has now replaced analysis as the central concern of the campuses. And not just advocacy, or spirited advocacy. Campus political advocacy is more than passionate. It is ferocious. It has no time for quibbles about pros and cons of different viewpoints, but aims to stamp out all opposition to a campus orthodoxy. It is completely closed-minded and intolerant, and vicious toward those who disagree.

In an earlier time, the difference between the political street and the academy with respect to political ideas was that the first dealt in advocacy and the second in analysis, but now the difference is that the political street deals in advocacy while the campus deals in *violence-backed* advocacy. Instead of being the reasoned antidote to everyday politics, the academy is now a more extreme version of it.

A common defense of these highly unpleasant campus incidents is that they are isolated cases not representative of higher education in general. That defense no longer works when it's clear that the same thing is happening all across the country, in public institutions as well as private ones, in small liberal arts colleges just as in large research-oriented campuses, in fairly obscure institutions just as in the nation's most prestigious campuses. It's no longer possible to deny that we are dealing with a pervasive nationwide campus culture.

• • •

Before we reach any overall judgment of these events we need to ask: who is really doing this? In the aftermath of the riot at UC Berkeley some attempted to blame agitators from off campus. But the repetition of such incidents on one campus after another soon destroyed that particular excuse. Students are usually found to be on the frontlines, which has led to an assumption that it's mostly a matter of inexperienced young people acting up. But students who were behaving badly on their own account would soon have been set straight by faculty and administration, and order would quickly have been restored. Pushback from those quarters is generally notable for its absence, however. If and when there is any at all, it is usually late, and minimal. Moreover, students were just as young and inexperienced fifty years ago, and they didn't show this appalling closed-mindedness then.

Today's students must have gotten those resolutely closed minds from somewhere, and it's not hard to figure out the most likely source: their teachers. And indeed, a series of parallel campus incidents involving mainly faculty and administration supports this conclusion. These incidents leave no room for doubt as to the real source of the problem.

In the fall of 2017, Bruce Gilley, a professor of political science at Portland State University, published an article in the *Third World Quarterly* with the title: "The Case for Colonialism." Gilley argued that whatever the motives of the colonialists, they had improved many lives, while the regimes that took their place have done a great deal of damage. The essence of his argument is contained in this sentence: "The notion that colonialism is always and everywhere a bad thing needs to be rethought in light of the grave human toll of a century of anti-colonial regimes and policies."

Gilley was of course far from the first writer to note that colonial regimes had often been the means by which the benefits of a more technologically and politically advanced culture were spread to other cultures. His article was a careful exercise in weighing the negative against the positive effects of colonialism, which is a perfectly normal form of academic analysis. It has always been clear that there was at least something to be said on both sides of the ledger. How could it be otherwise in complex human situations?

But Gilley's essay caused an enormous uproar. A petition demanding that the article be withdrawn gained more than ten thousand signatures. The attack on the essay was extraordinarily bitter and Gilley himself was vilified. The organizers of the petition were faculty, not students. Fifteen members of the editorial board of the journal in which the article was published resigned. Because the editor received death threats, Gilley agreed to the withdrawal of the article, though without recanting what he had said. (He published it again later in *Academic Questions*, the journal of the National Association of Scholars.) The response to Gilley's article was fully the equivalent of a shout-down and silencing of a speaker, done this time by very large numbers of his fellow professors. They insisted not only that he was wrong, but that he had no right to publish his opinion, or even to hold it.

What is important here is the particular way in which they expressed their disagreement with him. Academic people—professors and researchers—used to have a standard way of proceeding when they wanted to disagree with an argument like Gilley's. They would have examined Gilley's account of the benefits that colonialists brought to colonized countries, in order to show that he had exaggerated or misstated them; and then they would similarly have rebutted his account of the evils of postcolonial rule. That would allow them to argue that his general conclusion about colonialism was wrong because he had overestimated the positive effects and underestimated the negative ones.

That is the genuine professorial way of arguing: by careful analysis, with judicious use of relevant facts. But that's not what Gilley's opponents did. They wanted nothing to do with academic analysis. They began and ended with the political judgment that colonialism was evil, period. They would not permit anyone to say anything that was positive about colonialism, regardless of any facts whatever that might be called on to support it. Anything but a 100 percent negative judgment was strictly forbidden. Did India get railways, a common language that united the country, and democracy from the British—in addition to the hardships of colonial exploitation? You must not say it or even think it. The colonialists' motives were evil, therefore every single aspect of their influence on a colonized country must be seen as evil, period. No argument or evidence to the contrary can be allowed, anywhere, anytime. Gilley had weighed the positive against the negative effects of colonialism, but his opponents said, in essence: you may only condemn colonialism.

What was truly astonishing about this episode was that here were literally thousands of people with professorial appointments who completely rejected the very idea of academic thought and analysis. They were so fully in the grip of a political animus that they would not allow anyone who didn't share their political viewpoint to be heard. Their political zealotry was making them unable to think and behave as all professors should do. Their mental world was limited to what their political outlook dictated and what might advance their political goals. Political radicals are harshly critical of their own society, and they rate colonialism as among the most grievous of its sins. For them, historical fact can never be allowed to complicate or interfere with that fiercely held political opinion.

It is the job of academics to investigate such questions as how the more advanced cultures have spread technological, medical, and political innovations to less advanced cultures, often through conquest. Scholarly research must look carefully at complex historical situations that are always made up of many different strands, and must do full justice to all the factors at play. But the mob that went after Gilley had no interest in historical understanding. Their thought stopped dead with the political judgment: *colonialism is bad!* Radical politics stopped academic thought before it could even begin. What Gilley's opponents demonstrated is that political radicals can't be true academics, and yet here we saw thousands of them employed as professors in spite of their having no interest whatsoever in academic analysis and thought.

Gilley's case didn't get nearly as much public attention as the UC Berkeley riot did, but it was actually far more important, because it got to the heart of the problem on the campuses. The sheer number of professors involved showed that the betrayal of reasoned debate and scholarship was definitely not the work of an atypical few. On the contrary, very large numbers of college teachers were now so politically obsessed and so bitterly intolerant of other political stances that they could never provide the careful analytical thought and research expected of professors. This is the real source of the political obsession and mulish intransigence among students that resulted in the riots at UC Berkeley.

A number of similar incidents have reinforced the conclusion that campus closed-mindedness originates with college faculty who no longer behave like academics. They were clearly the driving force in the denunciation of Amy Wax, a distinguished University of Pennsylvania law professor. She and her University of San Diego colleague Larry Alexander published an article entitled "Paying the Price for Breakdown of the Country's Bourgeois Culture" in the *Philadelphia Inquirer* (August 9, 2017). Wax and Alexander recommended a return to some traditional values for groups that were currently in trouble:

> Get married before you have children and strive to stay married for their sake. Get the education you need for gainful employment, work hard, and avoid idleness. Go the extra mile for your employer or client. Be a patriot, ready to serve the country. Be neighborly, civic-minded, and charitable. Avoid coarse language in public. Be respectful of authority. Eschew substance abuse and crime.

Off campus these prescriptions might seem rather obvious, but Wax and Alexander went on to spell out what all of this meant in a way that challenged the bedrock political beliefs of their radical faculty colleagues:

> The loss of bourgeois habits seriously impeded the progress of disadvantaged groups.... Would the re-embrace of bourgeois norms by the ordinary Americans who have abandoned them significantly reduce society's pathologies? There is every reason to believe so. Among those who currently follow the old precepts, regardless of their level of education or affluence, the homicide rate is tiny, opioid addiction is rare, and poverty rates are low.... But restoring the hegemony of the bourgeois culture will require the arbiters of culture—the academics, media, and Hollywood—to relinquish multicultural grievance polemics and the preening pretense of defending the downtrodden.

In the context of the prevailing campus climate of political radicalism this was certainly provocative, but it was a point of view that needed to be reckoned with and countered with reasoned argument. Instead, the response was howls of outrage and an attempt to silence a heretic. An open letter signed by thirty-three of Wax's departmental colleagues—about half of the faculty of the formerly well-regarded University of Pennsylvania law school—did not debate or contest the issues, in the academic way. Instead it "condemned" what she and her colleague had said, and went on to suggest that it was so intolerable that it might justifiably have cost her her job had she not had tenure: "Wax has every right to express her opinions publicly free from fear of legal sanction thanks to the First Amendment, and she may do so without fear for her job due to her position as a tenured faculty member at Penn." This was also a strong warning to junior faculty without tenure that they had better not try saying such things. Worse still, the letter called upon students to inform on Wax, saying that if they heard expressions of "bias or stereotype" at Penn Law, "something has gone wrong, and we want to know about it." Next, a letter signed by fifty-four graduate students and graduate degree holders piled on, accusing Wax of racism, bigotry, white supremacy, and hate speech. They even called on the university's president to investigate her—and all for expressing an opinion that surely is widely held by ordinary people of good will throughout the nation.

Once again, it was Wax's faculty colleagues who began this inquisition. The students were following, not leading. And soon enough, the administration joined the mob too. Wax's dean told her that she would no longer be allowed to teach the introductory course that she had been teaching for some time. This happened to be a course for which Wax had recently received a prestigious award when her students were highly enthusiastic about her teaching. The grievous loss to students didn't matter to the mindlessly ruthless enforcers of political correctness. The dean punished Wax even though in so doing he punished the students who should have had continued access to the same splendid award-winning teaching experience that their predecessors had had. To any unbiased observer, of course, it was the dean who deserved to be disciplined—for pandering to the hysteria of his radical faculty.

Just as in Gilley's case, something was missing here that we had every right to expect from academic people. Professors who wanted to disagree with Wax would formerly have looked hard at the case she made and brought forward contrary evidence to show that she was wrong. For example, they might have tried to contest the factual link she made between poverty and having children before marrying. But once again, large numbers of people who held the title of professor showed themselves unwilling or unable to think and behave like a professor. They didn't contest her argument or her evidence, because what drove their condemnation of Wax had nothing to do with academic analysis. Their outrage was about her challenging a sacred cow of campus political radicalism, in this instance the rigid belief that the sad state of the black underclass is caused by society's racism, and by that alone. On campus, that is an article of faith not open to debate. As a genuine (and courageous) academic thinker, Wax tried to open it up to debate. By their punitive response, her colleagues betrayed the fact that they are radical political activists first and last, not academic thinkers, though they now constitute about half of the Penn Law faculty.

In Wax's case, the radical faculty took the lead and the administration then joined in. Sometimes, however, administrators take the lead, because they can always be quite sure that there will be substantial faculty support for their acts of political bullying and censorship. Such was the case at the Duke Divinity School. A member of the faculty, Anthea Portier-Young, was part of a campus committee on "Faculty Diversity and Inclusion." She decided to invite all divinity school faculty to attend a racial sensitivity training workshop.[2] But in the invitation she didn't merely explain descriptively the scope of what she was planning; on the contrary, the language she used made it clear that the whole exercise prejudged matters that are in fact highly controversial, and took propositions that were far from settled as incontrovertible truth. Even after all the progress that has been made in recent decades, she claimed that "racism is a fierce, ever-present, challenging force," and went on to say that the event would provide training in understanding both "historical and institutional racism."

In an age when firm institutional commitments to affirmative action are widespread, the notion of "institutional racism" is certainly subject to question. It generally involves the assumption that any statistical discrepancy in representation by race must be proof of racism, no matter what other factors might be at work. Thus, disproportionate numbers of black men in jail must be due to racism, regardless of possible differences in rates of criminal behavior. People who stage racial sensitivity training sessions invariably regard the allegedly undiminished presence of racism in our society as settled truth, which, strictly as a factual matter, it is not. Opinions vary a great deal about this, and it is pointless to pretend that they do not, and foolish to insist that others be forced to join in that pretense, as was being done here.

In response to the invitation, Professor Paul Griffiths (Warren Professor of Catholic Theology) noted that Portier-Young's wording reflected ideological commitments more than facts. He encouraged his colleagues not to attend, in part because "Events of this sort are definitively anti-intellectual. (Re)trainings of intellectuals by bureaucrats and apparatchiks have a long and ignoble history." He suggested that such exercises had "illiberal roots and totalitarian tendencies." This view of racial sensitivity training is certainly common enough, and so it's understandable that many people would be reluctant to attend meetings where speculative claims would be presented as if they were indisputable fact. They could be certain that any attempt to engage in reasoned discussion of those matters would itself be denounced as racism—not a pleasant prospect.

What Griffiths said here was simply a common view of these racial sensitivity workshops, yet he was bitterly attacked, and this time the attack came from a senior administrator. It was the dean of the divinity school, Elaine Heath, who launched the overheated accusation that Griffiths was guilty of "racism, sexism, and other forms of bigotry." Dean Heath sent a copy of her reprimand to every member of the school, an action which violated a longstanding rule of administration everywhere: when deans reprimand members of their faculty, they must do so in confidential letters addressed only to the person reprimanded, and only after due process.

A conscientious faculty colleague, Thomas Pfau, pointed out the obvious: that nothing in Griffiths' letter could remotely be said to express "racism, sexism, and other forms of bigotry," and that it was intellectually dishonest to say so. What Griffiths had said should be respected as a legitimate exercise of judgment and expression, Pfau observed. Undeterred, the dean doubled down. She initiated disciplinary action against Griffiths, and Professor Portier-Young filed a grievance against him too. Heath and Portier-Young both seemed determined to prove that Griffiths had been absolutely correct in seeing "totalitarian tendencies" in the kind of event that was planned. Their message was essentially: think as we do, or be punished. Griffiths soon resigned in disgust.

It's no exaggeration to say that Gilley, Wax, and Griffiths were persecuted precisely because they did what responsible members of the faculty must always do: all three spoke truthfully and intelligently at some risk to themselves. All of them seized on an issue of fundamental importance and expressed a well-crafted opinion that they knew would be unpopular on campus. They challenged campus orthodoxy with a badly needed corrective. Anyone who looked at what the three did from the perspective of the uncorrupted academy of the past would surely think these are first-rate academics—articulate, penetrating, and courageous. Would that all faculty behaved in this exemplary way! But it was precisely their academic excellence that made campus radicals single them out for punishment. The intellectual pygmies of the campus were ganging up on its intellectual giants.

• • •

We can be sure that the various forms of ruthless suppression of wrong opinion on campus (shout-downs, public humiliations, administrative punishments) originate with radical college faculty, are learned from them by students, and are reinforced by the senior administrators whose appointments they now control. But even without any overt actions by deans in support of radical malfeasance, it would still be obvious that administrators are complicit in it. Whenever student mobs have done their worst, the administration's failure to respond adequately is always conspicuous. The reason for this is obvious: while they may not share the protesters' methods, they do have the same judgments and attitudes. After the UC Berkeley riot of February 2017, the statements made by campus administrators always made it very clear that they shared the violent demonstrators' extreme hostility to the invited speaker.[†]

The events at Middlebury College, when Charles Murray and his

---

† Chancellor Nicholas Dirks of UC Berkeley sounded more like a hotheaded student radical than the chief campus officer of a major university when he addressed a message about Milo Yiannopoulos to the campus: "In our view, Mr. Yiannopoulos is a troll and provocateur who uses odious behavior in part to 'entertain,' but also to deflect any serious engagement with ideas. He has been widely and rightly condemned for engaging in hate speech....Mr. Yiannopoulos's opinions and behavior can elicit strong reactions and his attacks can be extremely hurtful and disturbing....[W]e urge anyone who is concerned about being targeted by Mr. Yiannopoulos to consider whether there is any value in attending this event...." So much for any concern about diversity of political opinion on the UC Berkeley administration's part. It is Dirks himself who is more obviously guilty of wanting to "deflect any serious engagement with ideas" by making a personal attack.

colleague from the Middlebury faculty were physically attacked, likewise showed us where the administration stood. Professor Alison Stanger needed to be hospitalized after she was attacked, and that posed a serious problem for the college administration. They could not escape their responsibility to do something about violent thuggery on campus when it had gone so far. Accordingly, Middlebury's president was compelled to promise real disciplinary action. But when penalties were eventually announced many months later, not a single student was either suspended or expelled. Most got probation; a few got "college discipline," which meant a note in the student's file. This gentle slap on the wrist was deemed appropriate even when physical violence had resulted in a hospitalization. Murray justifiably described the disciplinary process as a farce: it had sent the message that you can violently assault speakers you disagree with and nothing will happen to you. And the public noticed this pusillanimity. Why did Middlebury administrators expose themselves to public ridicule in this way? There can be only one explanation: they feared their radical faculty more than they feared the public. Had student radicals been expelled, faculty radicals would certainly have turned on the administration.

It seemed a hopeful development when a little over a hundred Middlebury faculty signed a statement of principles that included the key phrases: "No group of professors or students has the right to act as final arbiter of the opinions that students may entertain; no group of professors or students has the right to determine for the entire community that a question is closed for discussion." But two-thirds of the faculty refused to sign the statement. The distribution by department was even less encouraging. Three-quarters of the geology faculty signed, but in the large humanities departments (e.g., history and English) the proportion was around one-quarter. Let's be clear about this: three-quarters of these large departments that were once the conscience of the American campus refused to express their disapproval of violent physical attacks on speakers. In the sociology department things were still worse: only 15 percent signed. In the heavily politicized "Studies" departments (e.g., Afro-American Studies, Feminist Studies) not a single member of the faculty signed. That's right: every single member of the faculty in these departments evidently had no objection to beating up people with whom you have intellectual disagreements.

The pattern that emerges here is one we'll find again and again: the degradation of campus life has been concentrated mainly in the humanities and social sciences, but has a 100 percent presence in the newer "Studies" departments devoted to race and gender. The statement of principles signed by one-third of the Middlebury faculty seemed encouraging only until one realized what it really implied: that fully two-thirds of the faculty were on the other side. The thugs who had attacked Murray and his colleague thus had substantial faculty support—a fact which explained the administration's passivity.

That a fairly large minority of the Middlebury faculty still cared about genuine academic values is certainly an important fact of the situation, but unfortunately it is not one that should reassure us about the future of the campuses. As we'll see in the next chapter, the numbers of faculty who share that perspective are declining nationwide, and there are good reasons to believe that they will continue to dwindle with each passing year. And the smaller this group becomes, the harder it will be to accomplish any reform.

What needs to be reformed is not just the attitude toward free speech in campus public spaces. The incidents of more direct action by radical faculty tell us that the mistreatment of visiting speakers by students is only a symptom of a deeper problem. Even if we could stop the shouting down of invited guests on campus, that would not change what is happening in the classrooms—the places where the great majority of campus lectures take place. The same closed-minded instructors would still be there, preaching the same contempt for ideas that they don't like. There is no need to shout down opposing views in those classrooms when activist instructors will just exclude them from their lectures and reading lists. While shout-downs get the public's attention, the suppression of opinion on campus is far more pervasive than that: a controlling majority of the faculty vehemently oppose a wide spectrum of political ideas and will not tolerate them either in classrooms or in public spaces. Censorship of ideas that offend campus orthodoxy happens long before it becomes visible at public lectures by visiting speakers, and that is why students have learned to shout those ideas down. What has made this censorship feasible is a systematic pattern of one-party appointments to the faculty over many years. When the great majority of the faculty speak in only one way, an ever-smaller minority become increasingly unwilling to risk persecution by speaking in opposition.

If certain ideas are banned, that is done to protect other ideas: these are the two sides of the coin of censorship. The ideas that are protected by this censorship are those of the people who now dominate the campus. It matters not one bit to them that universities have always been places where ideas are examined and analyzed; while they are in control, their own ideas will be advocated and promoted, but not analyzed. These are the ideas of the radical left, but what is most zealously protected is a subset of those ideas. In all the campus incidents that I've mentioned so far, the underlying issues have generally been much the same.

Take first the shout-down of Heather Mac Donald. What provoked the anger of the campus protesters was her research into the question whether police especially target black men for arrest and even killing. Mac Donald looked at the relevant statistics and concluded that "if there is a bias in police shootings, it works in favor of blacks and against whites. Officers' use of lethal force following an arrest for a violent felony is more than twice the rate for white as for black arrestees, according to one study. Another study showed that officers were three times less likely to shoot unarmed black suspects than unarmed whites."[3] This enraged the campus mob because the belief system of faculty radicals requires that our society be judged still as racist as ever, which means that police *must* be targeting black men, whatever the evidence may say. That belief simply may not be questioned. We need not and should not even look at evidence. If Mac Donald questions the belief in undiminished, systemic racism, she is by that fact alone a proven racist, and must be silenced.

The attack on Paul Griffiths proceeded from the same rigidly held belief that racism is still rampant in our society. Any questioning of this belief is thought to justify compulsory racial sensitivity training for everyone. But Griffiths sinned both by questioning the dogma that racism in our society is as bad as ever, and by challenging the incoherence of racial sensitivity programs. The response was, essentially: you are not allowed to say that on campus.

Charles Murray's manhandling at Middlebury College raised the same issue. Murray had previously written about persistent ethnic differences in IQ test scores,[4] and though he discussed many different explanations of those discrepancies without committing himself firmly to any one of them, the fact that he had even looked into this question offended against the bedrock beliefs of political radicals. For them, the only possible explanation for statistical differences between blacks and other races is the enduring racism of our society; no other explanation may be looked at or evaluated. Anyone who examines other explanations of the discrepancies between the races in IQ scores must be a racist and therefore must be shut down.

Wax and Alexander sinned in an especially grievous way, because they described a list of behaviors and habits that minorities ought to adopt in order to enhance their material well-being in our society. And their list was an eminently reasonable one. But the clear implication of their essay was that blacks could improve their situation by changing their behavior, which in effect challenged the unshakable campus radical belief that differences in the circumstances of blacks and whites can only be attributed to continuing racism.

The same logic is applied to possible differences between the sexes. Christina Hoff Sommers' lecture at Lewis and Clark College on May 5, 2018 was shut down with the claim that she was a "known fascist," because she had said that "personal preference, not sexist discrimination, plays a role in women's career choices," and that "not only do women favor fields like biology, psychology, and veterinary medicine over physics and mathematics, but they also seek out more family-friendly careers." With respect to matters of the sexes, the campus radical's immutable truth is that any and all differences in the present status of men and women can only be due to the sexism of our society, because men and women are not different. If you think that women have different interests or abilities, you are a sexist, and you must be shut down.

Bruce Gilley offended campus orthodoxy by looking at the historical evidence of the effects of colonialism, good and bad. In the eyes of the radical faculty, colonialism is evil, period, and you may not say anything that in any way qualifies that basic truth. This belief is largely a branch of the radical obsession with the idea of racism in our society, of which ubiquitous colonialism is seen as another manifestation.

It's certainly true that speakers have also been disrupted for no other reason than that they are identified as conservatives: Ben Shapiro and David Horowitz are shouted down on that account. But what most provokes the determination to silence speakers is any challenge to the radical insistence that racism and sexism remain pervasive in our society.

$$\bullet \quad \bullet \quad \bullet$$

Censorship on college campuses concerning questions where the opinions of thoughtful people differ is contrary to what we have always thought about higher education. Until recently, universities dealt in precise argument using evidence that is systematically gathered and carefully analyzed—not in ruthlessly enforced uniformity of opinion based on arbitrary political dogma. That is exactly the kind of anti-intellectual behavior that we expect universities to remedy—it's what we have them for. If those institutions now routinely resort to this irrational thuggery, what is the point of them? We already see enough of that in the wider world. Academics who behave in this way are really telling us not only that *they* don't do university-level thinking, researching, or analyzing of issues, but that they won't allow anyone else on campus to do it either. They betray the institutions that employ them and make a mockery of their professorial titles.

It is of course a sign of weakness, not strength, when faculty radicals banish from campus anything that might compete with their cherished beliefs. They seem to understand that their dogmas need to be protected by shutting down debate because without that protection they might not survive. Critics of today's campuses talk of students as "snowflakes," but the real snowflakes here are the ideas of campus radicals: too fragile to survive unrestricted debate. The safe spaces that radicals really want to create are safe spaces for their ideas. Take again the case of colonialism: the facts that Bruce Gilley assembles about the miserable state of some postcolonial societies are utterly devastating, and campus radicals respond by making sure that those facts are buried. But that is an admission that they have no way of answering them.

It's easy to see why the ideas of campus radicals need to be protected when we consider how they fare in the wider world. There they soon look completely foolish. The idea that there could not possibly be any differences either of temperament or of aptitude between men and women is protected by temper tantrums on campus, but in the real world most people think it very silly indeed. The rigidly enforced campus shibboleth that our society is still as racist as ever seems completely out of touch with reality just as soon as we leave the campus: in the real world, employers everywhere are desperately trying to hire more minorities. The facts that Heather Mac Donald assembles to show that police don't target black men are overwhelming, but even without them most people easily see that police today are visibly anxious never to be accused of treating black men unfairly. And as to colonialism, everyone in the real world beyond the campus walls can see, for example, that Robert Mugabe's long rule has devastated Zimbabwe to an extent that colonialism never came close to; only someone blinded by ideological hatred could fail to see it.

If their beliefs are picked apart with great ease in the outside world, the radicals make quite sure that this can't happen on campus. This arrangement creates a fantasy world, a radicals' paradise in which things that everyone in the real world knows to be false can be true, and indeed the only permissible truth. It is a rarified world in which there can never be any question that hardline socialism really works or that Karl Marx's ideas have survived the test of historical experience unscathed, that affirmative action programs never have problematic side effects, that cops are by nature racists, that the rich never did anything to earn or deserve their wealth, that middle-class America is still as racist as ever, that men and women are indistinguishable, and so on. It is a world in which radicals can luxuriate in the confidence of their own virtue and wisdom, safe behind a wall that separates them from the reality that is kept out of the campus. Here, dead or dying ideas are propped up so that everyone on campus can pretend that they still live. Students become the frontline enforcers of this fantasy world, and in that role some of them become ugly little bullies, not snowflakes. Unfortunately, this fantasy world is built on the ruins of what used to be universities.

What are the intellectual resources that the radical campus

substitutes for evidence and argument? The sum total of its analysis, thought, and judgment appears to consist in the employment of a few key words that, as we have already seen, are used indiscriminately in almost any context: fascist, bigot, racist, sexist, white supremacist. These words are all designed to stop analytical thought before it can even begin. If one were to take them away from campus radicals they would be helpless—yet our campuses are now largely controlled by such intellectually stunted people. Of course there are still some serious thinkers on the campuses, mainly concentrated in scientific and technological fields, but control of the campuses is now definitely not in their hands. A radical sect has colonized and finally taken over a precious national resource for its own selfish purposes. In so doing, it is depriving society of something that in the past has been crucial to its success.

We have always expected universities to teach students to think in a careful, well-considered way: to study what previous thinkers have had to say about any given issue, and to examine all the available evidence before reaching a conclusion. I'll call this *disciplined* thinking—thinking that lets itself be guided by the direction in which evidence and reasoned analysis of that evidence points, regardless of what our initial sympathies might have been, or what our political interests may be. Judged by this standard, the radical campus is a fraud, and a betrayal of everything that a university should be. Whenever evidence, analysis, or simply intellectual curiosity might undermine the radical party line, they are pushed aside. It is sobering to remember that in the past we sent our children to college so that they could learn *not* to do this, because that was what *uneducated* people were more likely to do. Now those bad habits are not corrected, but instead reinforced.

Rethinking everything is the essence of academic life: what we expect from universities is the cultivation of open-mindedness and intellectual curiosity. But an orthodoxy has taken hold on the campuses, and any attempt to rethink it is forbidden because politics trumps genuine intellectual activity.† Political sympathies are of course present in any human institution, and not in themselves inimical to disciplined

---

† Radicals would probably say in response that their views result from rethinking older orthodoxies, but even if true, that could never justify the reimposition of a new orthodoxy; on the contrary, it only shows that all orthodoxies need to be treated with skepticism.

thinking. It is only a certain kind of politics that is routinely allowed to trump analysis and evidence: radical politics, the kind that has finished with thinking and is only interested in finding a means of implementing its beliefs.

Left-wing sympathies don't necessarily trump disciplined thought, and a story involving my University of California colleague Richard Sander, now a professor of law at UCLA, illustrates the difference. From very early in his career, Sander had a serious interest in black advancement and racial justice. He worked for social reform, but was always careful to keep an eye on unintended side effects of any reform measures that might seem beneficial. When he took a faculty post at UCLA's law school he began to look into the effects of racial preferences in law school admissions. He formulated a straightforward question: What impact did preferences for blacks in law school admissions have on the number of black lawyers in our society? The intent of preferences was to enlarge that number, but what was the result?

Sander set out to find the facts, and this is where disciplined thinking is crucial. He would have been delighted to find that preferences in admissions increased the number of black lawyers in our society. To his chagrin, he found that it was the other way around: there would be more black lawyers *without* the preferential policies. The reason was that too many black law students were being placed in academic environments that didn't match the educational level they had reached, and so they became discouraged and dropped out. The "mismatch" effect was disrupting their educational progress and derailing their aims. Sander had followed the evidence where it led, which is what disciplined thinking does.

Sander noted that "strongly held beliefs about public policy could blind people on all sides of important issues to the actual state of affairs."[5] Indeed, while he kept his eye on the "actual state of affairs," campus radicals did not. They were annoyed that affirmative action was being questioned, and this emotional reaction trumped evidence and analysis. The atmosphere on campus with respect to Sander's research became toxic. Some people sent him private messages of support but didn't dare make their support public for fear of being vilified by the radical bullies. As news spread of what Sander was finding, absolutely *nobody* in authority registered any concern about the harm being done to black students by their policies. Too many people were too deeply invested in racial preferences. What they seemed to care most about was that their support of preferences signaled their own virtue.[6] Campus officials began to make it harder for Sander to get at the facts he needed for his research. If the facts didn't say what campus authorities wanted them to say, then the facts must be hidden.

Imagine for a moment what would have happened had someone discovered a flaw in Sander's research. He'd already shown that fact and analysis could move him in a different direction, and there is no reason to doubt that he would move in yet another direction if new revelations pointed that way. That's what disciplined thinkers do. By contrast, his opponents didn't care about the facts: they would continue to support affirmative action regardless. The absurd result is that administrators and faculty still take pride in a program that has now been shown to damage the students it is supposed to be helping. Walter Williams explains why they hold this position so firmly:

> To admit these students makes white liberals feel better about themselves. It also helps support the jobs of black and white university personnel in charge of diversity and inclusion. The question for black people is whether we can afford to have the best of our youngsters demeaned, degraded and possibly destroyed to make white liberals feel better about themselves.[7]

When Richard Sander began asking similar questions, he showed what disciplined thinking looks like. It's what we send our children to college to learn. But when they arrive today, they will get the exact opposite. If they already have some intellectual curiosity, and some commitment to letting evidence lead where it must, it will be knocked out of them. They will learn that certain beliefs are mandatory, and that any attempt to examine their coherence or factual basis will be punished. This is how far college campuses have sunk: far from teaching students how to think for themselves, they set out to make sure that those students never stray from campus groupthink. If they don't always succeed, that's only because some students are smart enough to see their professors for what they are: obsessed preachers of a radical political gospel, not genuine teachers. But this is no consolation. The best students can muster the intellectual strength to resist this miseducation, but they are still not learning any-thing, while the less able are getting a lesson in how not to think.

. . .

Threats and intimidation are an integral part of the reign of the closed-minded radicals. Anyone who speaks out against the rigid orthodoxy is a danger, and must be discouraged by being made an example of lest others follow suit. At the Duke Divinity School, Professor Griffiths was hounded into early retirement when he questioned the coherence and the motivation of racial sensitivity training. At Evergreen State College, there was no place on campus for Professor Bret Weinstein or his wife, Professor Heather Heying, after he refused to comply with demands that all white people leave campus for a day. At Yale University, Professor Nicholas Christakis was driven to resign his post as master of Silliman College and his wife, Erika, also resigned her teaching posi-tion after she questioned whether Halloween costumes needed to be policed for ideological correctness. At Harvard University, President Larry Summers was driven from office because when discussing possible explanations for low numbers of women in scientific fields he men-tioned, as one hypothesis among others, possible differences between men and women. All of these academic people raised intelligent ques-tions and were instantly made an example of so that the fragile campus orthodoxy could be kept free from challenge.

In the past, academic debates were always decided by the force of argument, not the weight of numbers. One of the most prominent signs of the current sickness of the academy is the appearance of letters and petitions, signed by very large numbers, attacking dissenters from radical orthodoxy. The hundreds of extra signatures add nothing to the cogency of an argument, and therefore can only be intended to intimidate, to shame, and to bully.

We can get a sense of how effective this intimidation has been from a blog posting by Scott Alexander, a psychiatrist, on May 23, 2018:

Here is a story I heard from a friend, which I will alter slightly to protect the innocent. A prestigious psychology professor signed an open letter in which psychologists condemned belief in innate sex differences. My friend knew that this professor believed such differences existed and so asked him why he had signed the letter. He said that he expected everyone else in his department would sign it, so it would look really bad if he didn't. My friend asked why he expected everyone else in his department to sign it, and he said "Probably for the same reason I did."[8]

For anyone familiar with the formerly uninhibited atmosphere of college campuses, where professors were expected to be provocative and even eccentric in their opinions, what Alexander recounts here is astonishing. Yet evidence of this extraordinary level of fear and intimidation is everywhere. When thirty-three of Amy Wax's Penn Law colleagues wrote a joint attack letter, one might well wonder what the other half of the department did. It's true that they didn't join in the attack, but they didn't speak up to defend her either. And that deafening silence—instead of a much-needed pushback against disgraceful intellectual thuggery—is just as much a defining feature of the radicalized campus as the verbal and physical assaults are.

There is no way to soften a judgment of all this: higher education is very sick indeed. Radical politics has poisoned it so completely that universities now behave like anti-universities. Instead of fact and analysis trumping politics, politics trumps everything. Many scientific and technological departments still give students a good education in their fields, but the entire range of departments that we used to think of as education for citizenship are now heavily corrupted.

The public is increasingly worried about what is happening on America's campuses. A study published in October 2018 by the organization More in Common found that 80 percent of Americans—four in five—now believe that "political correctness is a problem in our country." And since everyone knows that college campuses are the source of political correctness, that amounts to a resounding vote of no confidence in the campuses on the part of the general public. Another study done by Gallup in June 2018 found that "No other institution has shown a larger drop in confidence over the past three years than higher education."

Paradoxically, one of the things that have protected the radicalized campus for some time is its very absurdity. Many people who hear accounts of what is happening have a quite natural reaction: *You must be exaggerating.* How could this possibly have happened to our great universities? And that is a good question. How indeed is it possible that higher education in this country could have deteriorated so disastrously, and so quickly? In the next two chapters I'll try to answer this question. First, I'll set out exactly what has happened and who brought it about. Then, I'll show how it became possible for this to happen.

CHAPTER 2

Who Are the People Destroying Our Universities?

The situation we found in the previous chapter is both extreme and depressing, and it's natural to ask: How can this have happened to our once magnificent universities? Before we can understand *how* it happened, we need to have a clear sense of *what* has happened, and that in turn leads to the question of *who* has caused it. When we see professors ganging up on colleagues whose opinions they disapprove of, we might surmise that the root of the change on our campuses can be found in the composition of the faculty who now staff them. In fact it is radically different from what it used be, tilting much further left. Who are these people?

Apologists for the universities as they are today generally shrug their shoulders and say that academia has always leaned left, so nothing has really changed. But nothing could be further from the truth. There is much well-documented evidence to show that the change in the faculty over the last fifty years has been profound, and destructive to a degree that no one could ever have imagined.

Let's begin in 1969, when a survey done by the Carnegie Commission on Higher Education found that 45 percent of faculty had political views that were left or liberal, while 27 percent were middle-of-the-road, and 28 percent either moderately or strongly conservative. These numbers amount to a distinct but relatively mild tilt to the left, with both sides represented in numbers that were sufficient for a healthy debate between left and right on campus. Since then, many investigations of faculty political allegiance have been done, both by liberals and by conservatives. They have used different methodologies, the main difference being that some used voter registration data to determine party affiliation while others used self-reporting. Both methods have their drawbacks. Not all professors register to vote, and not all people who are asked about their party affiliation will consent to answer the question or will answer it truthfully. If we were only looking at any one particular survey, therefore, we should have to regard the answers it gives as no better than approximate. However, the pattern that emerges from numerous surveys of different kinds and over a considerable period of time is unmistakable.

Thirty years after the Carnegie survey, an enormous change had already occurred. In 1999 the political scientist Stanley Rothman, together with his co-authors S. Robert Lichter and Neil Nevitte, did a study of the political views of American professors and found that "a sharp shift to the left has taken place among college faculty in recent years."[1] What had been a mild tilt in 1969 became a very strong one within a generation: five left-of-center professors for every right-of-center one. And if we look more closely, things were actually much worse than they seemed on the surface. Many of the professors in the 1999 study were already faculty members in 1969, and their continuing presence on campuses would have diluted the hiring ratio of the intervening years. The skew of the new faculty hires in 1969–1999 must have been more than 5 to 1, then—at least 6 to 1, and probably more like 7 to 1.

But even these heavily skewed figures don't give us the full extent of the shocking bias in hiring over those thirty years. In addition to giving figures for the faculty as a whole, Rothman and his associates also broke them down by department. The left/right ratio in English departments had already become 88 to 3, and in political science it was 81 to 2. Those are departments where it is most important to have a range of social and political attitudes, because those attitudes are directly relevant to the substance of the department's work, but this is precisely where the tilt to one side had become so extreme by 1999 that it was already close to a virtual exclusion of the other. To put the matter another way, the tilt became the most extreme in those subject areas where the temptation is greatest for political activists to pack their departments with people who share their political agenda and exclude those who don't.

Departments such as English, history, and political science (among others) may be viewed as the departments that are central to education for citizenship, and by 1999 they were already close to being one-party departments. The only plausible explanation of the severe tilt in these departments is that a deliberate pattern of political hiring had targeted departments that are central to education for citizenship in order to pack them with leftists.

By 1999, the degree of the tilt was making it obvious to everyone. Campus liberals and radicals alike were accordingly becoming defensive about it. Some tried to argue that nothing had really changed because the campus had always tilted left, but everyone could see that the tilt was in fact much greater than in former years.

Another way of attempting to justify the sharp political tilt of campuses was to claim that it was simply the result of hiring by merit, in which conservatives fared badly because they were less intellectually open and flexible than their left-of-center colleagues. But this argument was fatally undermined by the alarming evidence that the faculty hired in recent decades were doing a poor job of educating their students. Employers were finding recent college graduates to be much less able to write and reason than their predecessors, and tests in general knowledge found them abysmally ignorant of their country's history and institutions. (More of this in a later chapter.) Colleges and universities in the past had evidently done a much better job of teaching than the more politically univocal one was doing. And as to intellectual flexibility, it is difficult to deny that few people are less intellectually open, flexible, and curious than a radical leftist.

Still another excuse for the heavily slanted campus was a claim that political conservatives were not really interested in becoming professors. Yet that wasn't the case in 1969, when large numbers of conservatives were professors, and there was no reason to suppose that conservatives as a group had suddenly become less interested in academic life. In any case, by 1999 it was clear that radicals were not hiring others like themselves reluctantly for want of conservative applicants; rather, they were hellbent on hiring fellow radicals.

What spoke most clearly against any of these attempts to explain away the newly huge political imbalance on campus was the subsequent surveys revealing that it was getting worse. It was hard to keep arguing that nothing had changed while an obvious change was still going on. It could never be convincing to invoke supposedly constant features of academic life, such as an alleged lack of appeal to the conservative temperament, when surveys kept showing that things were still changing at breakneck speed.

A survey conducted in 2006 showed that the pace of change was speeding up. It had taken thirty years for the quite benign 45 to 27 left/right ratio of 1969 to reach the much sharper 5 to 1, but it took only eight more years for it to reach an utterly disastrous 8 to 1. What explains this sudden acceleration? The answer is again not difficult to find. By the time that the campus left had achieved a 5 to 1 numerical superiority it was in a position to dominate the hiring process completely, and it was taking full advantage of that power. Politically based hiring could proceed at full steam.

Ironically, that survey in 2006 was conducted by two liberals, Neil Gross and Solon Simmons, who very much wanted to prove that the tilt was nothing like as bad as critics were saying. They claimed to have found a greater presence of moderate political opinion than was generally supposed.[2] A closer inspection of the data reveals that they had not.

Gross and Simmons used a very large sample of faculty from 927 different institutions. They asked each faculty member to self-identify as very liberal, liberal, slightly liberal, middle-of-the-road, slightly conservative, conservative, or very conservative. The resulting percentages for self-described liberals, ranging from "very" to "slightly," were 9.4, 34.7, and 18.1. The corresponding percentages for conservatives were 1.2, 8.0, and 10.5. The remaining 18 percent self-identified as middle-of-the-road. But Gross and Simmons then reduced these seven categories to three: liberal, moderate, and conservative. Both of the "slightly" groups were included in the moderates. This massaging of their data got the result they wanted: while liberals outnumbered conservatives by 5 to 1 (44.1 percent to 9.2 percent), they were themselves outnumbered by an even larger group of moderates, at 46.6 percent. This manipulated result seemed to be a refutation of the common criticism that the campuses were now completely left-dominated, and as such it was welcomed by academics and campus officials. But a deeper look into the details of their study shows that Gross and Simmons had actually found some-thing completely different.

They had relied on self-reporting, which is notoriously unreliable where claims of "moderation" are concerned. Most people like to think that they are moderates, flanked by extremists on both sides, but what feels like the middle on a heavily left-dominated campus will likely be left of center in the societal mainstream. In fact, Ilya Somin soon exposed the dubiousness of the study's "moderate" category by looking at data on voting in the 2004 presidential election. Since 21 percent of the faculty had voted for George W. Bush over John Kerry, and we can assume that the self-described conservative 19.7 percent voted for Bush overwhelmingly (if not exclusively), that leaves only a small number of Bush voters among the "moderates." Almost all of that group evidently voted for Kerry, while self-described moderates in the general popula-tion had voted for Kerry by only a 54-45 percent margin.[3]

But there was an even more compelling reason to conclude that Gross and Simmons had found a much more extreme tilt than they were willing to admit. The two knew that self-reporting was unreliable, and so they asked their respondents some questions designed to give a more objective way of measuring their political beliefs. They used a series of questions that make up what is known as the "Pew scale." On this scale, 5 is a perfect score on the political right and 1 a perfect score on the political left, with 3 being a dead-center score. Though this was a much more objective test that could therefore be used to correct for the subjective bias in self-reporting, Gross and Simmons did not actually use it to adjust their results from self-reporting. And it's easy to see why: because the story it told made complete nonsense of their reassuring claims that there were more moderates on campus than liberals.

The self-described middle-of-the-roaders in the Gross and Simmons study scored 2.2 on the Pew scale, while their solidly conser-vative group scored only 3.7. In other words, the people they claimed to be in the political center were on average slightly further to the left of dead center (3.0) than those deemed rock-solid conservatives were to the right of it. The discrepancy was even more shocking in their "slightly liberal" group, which scored 1.7 on the Pew scale—twice as far to the left of center as the so-called solid conservatives were to the right. Their

Pew score was in fact very close to that of the group self-identifying as solidly left. Yet Gross and Simmons included them in their "moderates." The group that claimed to be "slightly conservative" was in fact slightly liberal on the Pew scale, with a score of 2.8. There is no mystery about all this: on a heavily left campus, someone who is center-left will surely feel somewhat conservative alongside others. But the most stunning fact in the Pew scale results was that the self-identified solid liberals got an average score of 1.4, close to the perfect-left score of 1. Contrary to the reassuring message of moderation that Gross and Simmons tried to give us, fully 44 percent of the total faculty were extreme leftists, only 0.4 away from perfect left (and another 18 percent were only 0.7 from perfect left), while their solid conservatives on average were 1.3 points away from a perfect-right score.

Regardless of what Gross and Simmons claimed to have shown, what their data truly revealed was that the faculty in their sample were 9 percent conservative (though only mildly so on average), while 80 percent were solidly left, with well over half of those being extreme left. They had wanted to find that things were not as bad as conservatives claimed, but what they really found was that the strong move to the left that Rothman and his associates found in 1999 had accelerated. In a very short time, Rothman's overall 5 to 1 left/right ratio had become 8 to 1. Paradoxically, what gives the Gross and Simmons study added credibility is that they evidently did their best *not* to find what they really found. Campus spokesmen had dismissed earlier studies on the grounds that they were conducted by conservatives who had a stake in finding fault with the campus. The reverse was the case with Gross and Simmons. They did not expect to find what they found, did not want to find it, and then did their best not to see it. When Pew data that they collected to check the self-reporting results turned out to flatly contradict those results, Gross and Simmons just ignored the Pew data in their analysis.

But there was even more bad news in the Gross and Simmons study that undermined their attempt to reassure us that all was well. They found that one in five professors in the social sciences self-identified as "Marxist." (In the field of sociology the ratio was more than one in four.) Astonishing as this statistic is, it almost certainly understates the matter.

The word "Marxist" does not play at all well with the general public, and many whose mental framework has been largely formed by Marx's ideas prefer to describe themselves as "socialists" or "progressives," or simply "activists." We can assume, therefore, that the real number of people motivated by Marx's ideas among social science professors is higher—anything up to double the Gross and Simmons number, but certainly a good deal more than one in five.

Whichever one of these figures we use for the presence of Marxist professors in the social sciences, these are astounding numbers. In the real world beyond the campus walls, Marxism is well on the way to being an obsolete system of thought, having been tried (almost always by force rather than through the choice of an electorate) in over twenty different countries during the period 1917–1990, and abandoned in almost all of them due to virtual economic collapse. Those countries where it still survives (North Korea, Cuba, Nicaragua, Venezuela) are known to be among the most miserable countries on earth. China is an odd and atypical case, a country that is still a Communist dictatorship even though it has learned that Marx's economic ideas don't work. And yet this thoroughly discredited system of thought enjoys a commanding presence among college social sciences faculty, while one of the two most enduring political philosophies of the Western world (conservatism), the choice of about half of U.S. voters, is virtually banned from campus—an utterly bizarre situation. John Stuart Mill's diagnosis (in the second chapter of his *On Liberty*) of the need for two parties is still as valid as it was when he wrote it: "In politics, again, it is almost a commonplace, that a party of order or stability, and a party of progress or reform, are both necessary elements of a healthy state of political life…. Each of these modes of thinking derives its utility from the deficiencies of the other."

It is safe to say that self-identified Marxists are no more than a tiny fraction of the general public of the United States, which means that there is a huge discrepancy between this very small group in the population and the very large one found among social science professors. (Gross and Simmons say their figures indicate that "self-identified Marxists are rare in academe today," a judgment that is virtually self-parody on their part.) The question arises: why should this group be so heavily overrepresented on college campuses? The answer must be that Marxist ideas have such a hard time of it in the real world that those who espouse them have fled to the campuses for sanctuary. Campuses protect them from the merciless test of reality. But that raises another question: why should universities be so interested in hiring thinkers whose minds are firmly closed to the lessons of experience? Their intellectual rigidity is the very opposite of the true academic's inquiring mind, so their presence in substantial numbers on campuses leads us to conclude that the faculty hiring process has been hijacked by those who sympathize with this moribund ideology.

As to the humanities, Gross and Simmons find that the numbers there of self-described radicals or activists are approximately equal to those in the social sciences—about one-quarter of the total—which suggests a roughly similar political situation in the two areas, the only difference being that humanist radicals seem even more wary of the term "Marxist" than are their social science counterparts.

Since Gross and Simmons covered 927 institutions, their study was large enough to be a good guide to the state of academia in general, but one might still wonder if the nation's most prestigious universities are perhaps doing somewhat better. That question was answered by a study of faculty political registration at UC Berkeley and at Stanford University published by Daniel B. Klein and Andrew Western in 2004.[4] Though this study was done a few years before that of Gross and Simmons, the results were already more extreme than the 8 to 1 left/right ratio that the latter found. The overall figure for UC Berkeley was 9.9 to 1, and for Stanford 8.9 to 1. The breakdown by subject area at Berkeley was especially interesting. In the professional schools, the ratio was 4 to 1, in the hard sciences and mathematics 9.9 to 1, in the humanities 17.2 to 1, and in the social sciences 21 to 1. This was essentially the same kind of skewing we saw earlier: the more it really matters to have a faculty with a range of social and political attitudes—in the humanities and social sciences—the less of it there actually is. The greater the motivation to pack a department with radical leftists, the more of such packing there is.

Klein and Western found something else that was even more sinister. They broke down their figures by professorial rank, which allowed them to separate the figures for younger, more recently hired faculty from those for older ones. Full professors are mostly older hires, associate and assistant professors more recent ones, the latter the most recent of all. The left/right party registration imbalance was 8 to 1 for full professors, but the figure for the two junior ranks taken together was an astonishing 49 to 1.

There are a number of highly disturbing implications in these numbers. The first is that as older professors retire, they are being replaced by a group whose political tilt is much more extreme, essentially to the exclusion of one side of the political spectrum. The second implication, an exceptionally important one, is that since these are campuswide numbers, including science and technology departments, there will soon be no difference between the various departments. All of them, not just the humanities and social sciences, will exclude right-of-center voices. Hitherto, it always seemed possible to take comfort in the fact that the sciences, at least, were not politicized. No longer: physics departments will soon be all politically left too.

Such was the situation in the middle of the first decade of this century. One might have hoped that as news of this appalling deterioration and politicizing of the campuses became known, some efforts would have been made to stop it from getting worse. But that never happened: the degradation was allowed to continue. Boards of trustees, college presidents, faculty senates—they all looked on and did nothing. It must have been obvious to all of them that the campuses were in crisis, and that an already horrendous situation was rapidly getting even worse, but they were all either too cowardly or too complicit to act. The relentless drive toward the completely one-party campus simply continued.

The most recent surveys, conducted in the last two to three years, have predictably found that the tilt to the left has increased still more. There were always two good reasons to believe that this would happen. The first was the large discrepancy found by Klein and Western between the left/right split for older professors and that for more recent hires. The second was that what had already happened was proof positive of a grim determination to achieve a perfect one-party campus on the part of those who were now in a position to make it happen. By now, the huge imbalance between the left and right on campus is known to everyone.

Most people understand how unhealthy this campus condition is. The campus radicals know all too well what is happening, and they are going ahead as fast as they can to make the imbalance even greater, because they don't care one bit about the intellectual health of the campuses, but only about cementing their own control.

A study published in 2016 documented the continuing deterioration into one-party systems. Mitchell Langbert, Anthony Quain, and Daniel Klein looked into the voter registration of faculty in five different fields at forty of the nation's leading universities, and here is what they found:

> We looked up 7,243 professors and found 3,623 to be registered
> Democratic and 314 Republican, for an overall D:R ratio of
> 11.5:1. The D:R ratios for the five fields were: Economics 4.5:1,
> History 33.5:1, Journalism/Communications 20.0:1, Law 8.6:1,
> and Psychology 17.4:1. The results indicate that D:R ratios have
> increased since 2004, and the age profile suggests that in the future
> they will be even higher.[5]

The overall ratio of 11.5 to 1 included emeriti professors, that is, professors who have retired. The ratio for currently serving faculty must therefore be higher still. The authors concluded: "our findings surely indicate that the ratio of voting-D to voting-R for active humanities/social-science faculty at all U.S. four-year universities has gone up markedly over the past ten years." To appreciate fully what this judgment really means, we must remember that the left/right ratio that they found to have skewed so much was already disastrous at the beginning of that ten-year period.

The imbalance has become so catastrophic that individual professors often comment on what they observe in their own subject areas. Nicholas Quinn Rosenkranz, a professor at Georgetown Law School, observed that faculties at elite laws schools are "overwhelmingly liberal." Of his own institution he said:

> We are a faculty of 120, and, to my knowledge, the number of pro-
> fessors who are openly conservative, or libertarian, or Republican
> or, in any sense, to the right of the American center, is three—three

out of 120. There are more conservatives on the nine-member United States Supreme Court than there are on this 120-member faculty. Moreover, the ideological median of the other 117 seems to lie not just left of center, but closer to the left edge of the Democratic Party. Many are further left than that.[6]

Up until about 2016, we commonly heard denials from the campuses that they were effectively one-party ecosystems where right-of-center voices were rarely heard. Those denials have now stopped. Instead, we now see an unashamed and quite open suppression of conservative voices. Perhaps this change is due to a realization that the denials now completely lack plausibility, or perhaps instead it represents a growing confidence that radical control is now complete enough that they no longer matter. In any case, it indicates that a tipping point has been reached.

Two years after Langbert, Quain, and Klein did their study of forty universities, Langbert published the results of a study focusing on elite liberal arts colleges.[7] He looked at tenure-track faculty in fifty-one of the top sixty-six colleges in the *U.S. News and World Report* ranking, and the results may shock the reader even after all that we have seen so far: "faculty political affiliations at 39 percent of the colleges in my sample are Republican free—having zero Republicans. The political registration in most of the remaining 61 percent, with a few important exceptions, is slightly more than zero percent but nevertheless absurdly skewed against Republican affiliation and in favor of Democratic affiliation." Looking at academic departments, Langbert found that 78.2 percent "have either zero Republicans, or so few as to make no difference." Across the sample, the mean ratio of Democrats to Republicans was 10.4:1, and when Langbert excluded the military academies at West Point and Annapolis (which *U.S. News* included in its ranking), the ratio was an astonishing 12.7:1. And it will only get worse, and worse again.

The decision makers on the campuses are evidently determined to keep moving toward zero right-of-center professors. The forces that moved the ratio from less than 2 to 1 in the 1960s to the 12+ to 1 shown in the latest surveys are still at work. Retiring faculty are being replaced by a younger group with a virtually exclusive leftward tilt—not because young people in general are monolithically radical, but because new faculty recruitment is deliberately selective for radical leftism, and has been for some time. Nobody with any influence on campus is calling for a change of course, or shouting "danger ahead," or crying out that this is intellectual suicide for colleges and universities. Nothing is being allowed to interfere with the creation of a fantasy world where radical leftist beliefs can reign as absolute truth, insulated from dissent and from disturbing commentary about their catastrophic results in the real world beyond the campus walls.

The alarming extent of the political imbalance shown by faculty surveys is confirmed by a different kind of evidence, namely, financial contributions made by university employees to political campaigns. Campus Reform found that of the $4,681,192.76 in political contributions made by University of California employees in 2017–18, no less than 97.46 percent went to Democratic candidates and causes.[8] This percentage is even more lopsided and dismaying than that shown by surveys of faculty political affiliation.

· · ·

I've already noted that part and parcel of this concentration of college faculty to the left has been a change in the character of campus leftism. As it has grown in numerical strength it has also become much more extreme, something easily seen in the large numbers of Marxist faculty, completely disproportionate to their numbers in the general population. But this drift to ever greater extremism is the predictable consequence of a one-party campus. In a letter to the *Wall Street Journal* on July 30, 2018, Teresa R. Manning remarked that in one-party departments "the radical is made mainstream and the mainstream is made marginal."

John Stuart Mill gave us the explanation of how this must inevitably happen in his classic essay *On Liberty*. Mill seized on the dangers of a one-party institution with two memorable remarks that explain much of what has happened to higher education. The first is from the second chapter of *On Liberty*, where he remarks that "He who knows only his own side of the case, knows little of that." The crucial point here is that you can't really understand the case for the left until you also understand equally well the case for the right, because each is a necessary part of the definition of the other. This means that professors in an all-left department will not even be able to give a competent account of their own political views, for as Mill put the point, "they do not, in any proper sense of the word, know the doctrine which they themselves profess." When everyone around is on the left side of the spectrum, even the teaching of leftist thought will become incoherent.

If leftist professors think they can fill the gap by presenting the right's case themselves, Mill has a crushing answer: "Both teachers and learners go to sleep at their post as soon as there is no enemy in the field." The student must therefore "be able to hear [the arguments] from people who actually believe them, who defend them in earnest, and do their very utmost for them. He must know them in their most plausible and persuasive form."†

Intellectual opponents not only keep you sharp and alert; they are essential in enabling you to understand your own position thoroughly by understanding the opposition as well. This used to be something that all professors lived by: it was second nature to them. A university department where this spirit is entirely lacking doesn't deserve a place in the academy. And it's especially true that a political science department with one half of the spectrum of political thought missing can't be considered a competent department—it's completely unfit to teach political science. People who want to pack their departments with ideological soulmates are political activists, not academics; genuine professors of politics would know that insulating themselves from their opponents is intellectual suicide. When some leftists claim that conservative positions are not intellectually based, they merely demonstrate Mill's point: they show that they know little about political science, with respect either to the left or the right, for both have very long and complex histories of discussion and analysis. In academic life, people who disagree with you

---

† This does not imply that only committed advocates may present and speak to leftist beliefs. To say that students must be able to hear arguments from people who do their utmost for them is not to say that it is the *only* way in which they must hear them, but simply that an environment where such people are excluded is an intellectually defective one in which thought will atrophy.

provide both a discipline for your own thinking and an indispensable spur to more and better thought.

The second of Mill's remarks that is relevant here is this: "it is in a great measure the opposition of the other that keeps each within the limits of reason and sanity." Here he puts his finger on an important factor in the campus left's slide into irrational extremism. Where there are no right-of-center voices to keep the left healthy, the result will inevitably be a much more extreme and self-indulgent political culture. When each side faces an effective opposition, intellectual leadership will flow to those who can put the strongest case for their own side, the one least vulnerable to the criticisms of the other. Poorly thought-out extreme positions will be pushed to one side because of the need to defend against the other side in the most effective way. But when there is no opposition, leadership will instead flow to the most extreme and exciting positions of the left—that is, to its least defensible versions. Wishful thinking can then proceed without check.

This explains why all political monocultures will sooner or later degenerate into incoherence. Mill's point here has the advantage of putting the emphasis where it really belongs: not on the right-of-center professors who are missing from an all-left department, but on the professors who are there. The exclusion of their intellectual opponents dooms them to incompetence. Nicholas Rosenkranz comments in Mill-like fashion on the current imbalance: "One result, unfortunately, is a certain lack of rigor. To be blunt, a kind of intellectual laziness can set in when everyone agrees. Faculty workshops fail to challenge basic premises. Scholarship becomes unreflective and imprecise."[9]

In their efforts to expand the frontiers of knowledge, genuine scholars must continually reevaluate *everything* as they come to terms with new evidence, new discoveries, and new theories. Sometimes, new developments can make them see everything they thought they already knew in a different way. But all of this sounds very foreign to the temperament of people who cling to an obsolescent political theory and refuse to reevaluate it no matter how badly it turned out to work in the real world. This is why the astonishingly lopsided left/right numbers are so important: to surround oneself with hugely disproportionate numbers of people who share the same political standpoint is a way to avoid rethinking, reevaluating, and responding to new evidence. An academy composed largely of people who can't and won't behave like academics is an empty shell.

But it's not just the concentration of one political viewpoint that corrupts academia. Making politics of any kind central to campus life must be damaging because the habits of mind of academic teachers are in so many ways the exact opposite of those of political activists. First of all, political motives will always stunt intellectual curiosity. In any worthwhile college education a student's mind must have the freedom to think afresh and to follow wherever facts or arguments lead. But that freedom of thought is constrained when its conclusion is fixed in advance by a political agenda. Students will never learn to think for themselves if their thought processes must always conclude by fitting into a predetermined belief system.

Second, political activism will always value politically desirable results more than the process by which conclusions are reached. In a college education and in academic research, those priorities must be reversed. In academia, thinking must never be constrained by considerations of the political desirability of the result.

Third, political activism wants action, while academic thought seeks understanding. Understanding a situation means looking hard at a whole complex of different factors that make it what it is, but political activism requires simplicity: a choice of this action rather than that. If action is allowed to rule over analysis, it will always cripple it.

But perhaps the most important difference between political activism and academic thinking is that they are polar opposites in the way they deal with alternative explanations. When a scholar begins to think that a difficult research problem can be solved in a particular way, he or she knows that the next step must be a careful look at all the plausible alternative explanations, to see if any of them works as well. And that process can't be perfunctory: each of those other possibilities must be given a sympathetic hearing. Genuine scholars know that they must do this if they are to develop new knowledge that will withstand the scrutiny of other experts in the field, and the test of time. And it's their job to instill this way of thinking in their students. But it's just in this crucial respect that political activists can't think and act like academics.

They have exactly the opposite attitude to alternative explanations and theories: they want to defeat them and have them go away, by any means possible. It's almost a psychological impossibility for them to give alternatives a sympathetic hearing.

The same incapacity can be seen when new evidence with respect to a particular social or political issue comes to light. The approach of an academically trained, disciplined thinker is to look immediately at how the new evidence might change the way we think about the issue in question: does it advance the case for one way of looking at it, while making others appear more doubtful? This is a mental process that a political activist can't go through, because his conclusion is already set in stone. His thought process will be limited by one simple reflex: how can he fit this new evidence into his existing mental framework without having to change anything of substance? For a real academic, unexpected new evidence is a challenge to rethink, and a valuable opportunity to do so, but the political activist is always too much the captive of his unshakable belief system to be able to use that challenge.

All these differences in mental habits, taken together, tell us that political activism will always undermine and corrupt academic thought. It's not just that political activists don't think like academics: they actually think in a way that is the polar opposite of academic thought. With political activists in charge of colleges and universities, as they are now, they won't just fail to provide a higher education: they will actually be destroying the capacity for analytical thought.

James Otteson gives yet another reason to keep political advocacy out of the campuses, noting how politics involves emotional allegiances that interfere with intellectual inquiry:

> Because politics is so fraught with emotion and tribal loyalties, it is extremely dangerous in the context of higher education. It replaces a loyalty to the process of inquiry with a loyalty to one's tribe. We judge arguments and even people not on their merits, but instead on the extent to which they conform to our prejudices or group identities. It therefore imperils our professional identities as academics if we allow politics to enter into our scholarship. We might have political allegiances in our capacities as citizens, but as

academics, our loyalty should be to the process of inquiry alone. That means we should have no academic departments or institutes whose primary purpose is to inform, affect, or advocate public policy.[10]

By implication, Otteson is recommending the disestablishment of all those departments that advocate for social justice—of which there are far too many in today's academy.

So far, I have documented a deliberate and relentless drive over many decades to make academia a political monoculture. And I've argued that giving academia a political purpose is to destroy everything that makes it what it ought to be, and what makes it valuable to our society. But the sad fact is this incompatibility between political motivation and the proper functioning of the academy had always been well known, as is evident from the many longstanding rules and regulations that were designed to protect universities from political influence and motivation. Which means that all who have taken part in the long drive to politicize academia knew very well that they were violating well-established professional norms, institutional rules, and even laws. They all knew that using the academy for a political purpose was improper but went ahead anyway. Their own selfish purposes came first regardless of the damage those purposes did to academia.

The most famous and still the most important statement on the importance of keeping political advocacy out of university teaching was made in 1915 by the American Association of University Professors (AAUP):

> The university teacher, in giving instruction upon controversial matters, while he is under no obligation to hide his own opinion under a mountain of equivocal verbiage, should, if he is fit for his position, be a person of a fair and judicial mind; he should, in dealing with such subjects, set forth justly, without suppression or innuendo, the divergent opinions of other investigators; he should cause his students to become familiar with the best published expressions of the great historic types of doctrine upon the questions at issue; and he should, above all, remember that his business is not to provide his students with ready-made conclusions, but to train them to think

for themselves, and to provide them access to those materials which they need if they are to think intelligently.... The teacher ought also to be especially on his guard against taking unfair advantage of the student's immaturity by indoctrinating him with the teacher's own opinions before the student has had an opportunity fairly to examine other opinions upon the matters in question, and before he has sufficient knowledge and ripeness of judgment to be entitled to form any definitive opinion of his own. It is not the least service which a college or university may render to those under its instruction, to habituate them to looking not only patiently but methodically on both sides, before adopting any conclusion upon controverted issues.

This statement instantly became the reference point for all future discussions of the dangers of using classrooms for political indoctrination. Rightly so, for it is indeed a brilliant summary of the issues. But in the present-day world of college campuses, it is as if that statement did not exist and had never existed. Its provisions are routinely flouted. Far from making sure that students are exposed to the "best published expressions of the great historic types of doctrine upon the questions at issue," college faculty are systematically emptying the classrooms of all but one political doctrine, that of the radical left. And far from "habituat[ing] them to looking not only patiently but methodically on both sides, before adopting any conclusion upon controverted issues"— the only true way for higher education—radical faculty are making sure that students hear one side only and pressing them to accept it without hearing any other. This alone constitutes a stunning collapse of the quality and integrity of higher education.

. . .

My concern in this book is primarily with the political corruption of higher education, but we can't ignore the fact that this use of academia for a political purpose also constitutes large-scale political cheating. Democracy itself is damaged by this abuse of higher education. When we see governments in Third World countries using the resources of the state to keep themselves in office, we generally disparage the countries concerned as banana republics, with all it implies about their lack of democratic institutions and practices. When governments use their control of state offices and of the educational system to make their reelection all but certain, they deserve the contempt expressed in that term. And that is equally true when political parties not currently in power abuse an educational system in order to get back into power. In a genuine democracy, elections are conducted on a level playing field. When one party uses its control of higher education to advance its cause, that is exactly the kind of conduct that we disparage in Third World countries.

It is safe to say that a legislature could never be asked to appropriate funds to promote one political party or philosophy at the expense of another without an immediate public outcry. And the same would happen if a state university were to ask for an appropriation of funds so that it could pursue progressive social change. Legislatures do not give money to universities so that they can pursue political goals. That kind of political change is sought at the ballot box, to which students and faculty have the same access as any other members of the public. Let's therefore be quite clear about this: when funds appropriated for education are used instead for political purposes, those funds are being stolen away from the use that they were appropriated for, and being used fraudulently for a purpose that they could never have been appropriated for.

Every minute of classroom time at a public university presupposes the expenditure of a good deal of public money. There is the construction, equipping, and maintaining of the building; the cost of the land; the salary and benefits of the instructor; and the costs involved in multiple layers of campus administration. Classroom time thus represents valuable public property created for a specific public use. An individual's political beliefs, on the other hand, are a private matter, and his or her wish to promote them is a private, not a public concern. The creation of a completely left-wing faculty is not something that was done for an educational purpose; it was done to further the private political beliefs of the people concerned. When publicly funded facilities are used for the private purposes of the individuals to whom they have been entrusted, that is in essence the converting of publicly owned resources to private use—in other words, stealing. We have no difficulty in recognizing that this has happened when, say, a piece of university equipment is stolen: that is clearly the conversion of property paid for with public funds to a private use. But when we compare these two cases, it is hard to distinguish them from a moral standpoint. In both, something that belongs to the public is taken by individuals for their own personal use. Should people who are essentially embezzling public funds be running our universities?

Both state and federal laws prohibit the use of public money or the paid time of public employees for partisan activity or for personal purposes not authorized by law. The federal Hatch Act provides that federal employees "May not use their official authority or influence to interfere with an election…[or] engage in political activity while on duty." In the state of California, the Government Code provides that "It is unlawful for any elected state or local officer, including any state or local appointee, employee, or consultant, to use or permit others to use public resources for a campaign activity, or personal or other purposes which are not authorized by law." What is prohibited here clearly goes beyond electioneering for a candidate for office and includes any kind of promotion of a political candidate, party, or cause. An individual's political stance is a "personal" matter that state funds may not be used to promote.

The longstanding recognition that universities must be protected from political influence or motivation is enshrined in rules and regulations of almost all universities that prohibit their use for political purposes. My own university (the University of California) has a long series of such policy statements. They not only prohibit political use of the university, but also explain carefully just why that is so, and how it would damage the university. Article IX, Section 9 of the California Constitution provides that "The University shall be entirely independent of all political or sectarian influence and kept free therefrom." A directive by President Clark Kerr in 1961 said that "University facilities and the name of the University must not be used in ways which will involve the University *as an institution* in the political, religious, and other controversial issues of the day." Another by President Charles Hitch in 1970 provided that "There are both educational and legal reasons why the University must remain politically neutral. Educationally, the pursuit of truth and knowledge is only possible in an atmosphere of freedom, and if the University were to surrender its neutrality, it would jeopardize its freedom." The latest version of the university's Academic Personnel Manual states that among the examples of unacceptable faculty conduct is "Unauthorized use of University resources or facilities on a significant scale for personal, commercial, political, or religious purposes."

All of these federal and state laws and university rules and directives are still fully in effect, as are comparable ones in other states. The AAUP statement about politics in the classroom still stands. It is still understood everywhere that making higher education subservient to politics is wrong and harmful. How do we know this? Because when challenged, the university teachers who are doing so almost always deny that they are doing any such thing. And this tells us that they know perfectly well that what they are doing cannot be defended. Yet everywhere, college faculty and administrators are flagrantly violating these well-known laws, regulations, and professional understandings about the need to keep universities free of political motivation.

What those rules were meant to prevent—the degradation of higher education—has now happened. Indeed, the present condition of college campuses has proved just how sensible and necessary all of those rules were. But how could the protection that so many different rules and regulations should have afforded fail so miserably? How could we have gone from the academia of the 1950s, when American universities were the envy of the world, to that of today, when a radical sect has all but destroyed their integrity? My next chapter turns to the sorry history of how it all happened, and how what had previously seemed ironclad safeguards failed so completely.

CHAPTER 3

How Was It Possible
for This to Happen?

We can summarize the major findings of the last chapter as follows: the political tilt to the left has now reached a degree not remotely matched in the past, in many areas so extreme that it amounts to exclusion of any but left-of-center faculty; the leftism now prevalent on campus is far more extreme than it is off campus; the more that politics is relevant to a field of study (the most obvious being political science and sociology), the greater the preponderance of left-wing faculty; and younger faculty members are more solidly left-oriented than older faculty, so that the degree of the tilt continues to grow as retirees are replaced by new appointments.

As one-party campuses have developed, they have become radicalized and their intellectual level has collapsed. How could this possibly have happened? Had anyone predicted fifty years ago the horrendous decline of our formerly splendid academic institutions and their virtual takeover by radical political activists—people with no real interest in academic thought, teaching, or research, who wanted instead to use their positions to promote their extreme political ideology—that person would have been laughed at. Almost everyone would have insisted: that's simply not possible. There were too many safeguards in the form of deans, appointment and promotion committees, a robust professional ethic, and well-known professional standards codified in institutional rules. In those days a young person who used his or her classroom to promote radical political views would soon be in the

dean's office and be told to shape up or be fired. Trustees, administrators, faculty—all were on the same page in this respect. Everyone
understood that political activism would be a serious threat to the
integrity of higher education.

How could people with no real interest in academic life have taken
it over so quickly and so completely? Why did all those safeguards prove
so ineffective? How could the watchdog committees and administrators
have let it happen? Why was such an unlikely group able to roll over
an institution that had seemed so staunch in its sense of its own values
and purposes? How was the academic world lost?

Though nobody would or could then have predicted this devastating
corruption of academia, there was already in 1962 a very small group
that had a well-formulated plan to do exactly what has now happened:
they were known as the Students for a Democratic Society (SDS). Yet
this was only a tiny group of around two hundred young people. It was
taken seriously by no one but its own members. They were largely college students who saw their own society as undemocratic and oppressive
because they were attracted to the Marxist ideas that then reigned in
the twenty or so Marxist dictatorships already known to be among the
unhappiest countries on earth—countries whose citizens, unlike the
members of SDS, were denied any part in choosing their own form of
government. SDS members were idealistic but ignorant and foolish,
seemingly knowing nothing of the evil being done in the name of the
ideas that they espoused. Understandably enough, nobody took these
earnest but gullible young people seriously. And yet the manifesto they
adopted at their first convention—held in Port Huron, Michigan—
described a plan that is almost identical to what has now happened to
our colleges and universities.

The "Port Huron Statement" began by holding America to be
morally responsible for poverty and malnutrition in the world, not the
governments of the relevant countries: "While two-thirds of mankind
suffers under nourishment, our own upper classes revel amidst superflu-
ous abundance." It went on to argue that democracy in America was a
sham: "Although mankind desperately needs revolutionary leadership,
America rests in national stalemate... its democratic system apathetic
and manipulated rather than 'of, by, and for the people.'" Nothing

could be expected from the American electorate because "For most Americans, all crusades are suspect, threatening." The correct solution would be socialism/Marxism: "the economy itself is of such social importance that its major resources and means of production should be open to democratic participation and subject to democratic social regulation."

The word "democratic" is here used twice in one sentence, from which we can certainly gather that it is an important idea for the writers, and yet they had already ruled out the ballot box as a means of getting to where they wanted to be. In fact they despaired of ever getting a majority of the American people to agree to what they wanted. Accordingly, "democratic" in their usage has nothing to do with rule by the people or their elected representatives. That's not what they envisaged. Instead, this appears to be the same use of the word once found in the name given to East Germany during the Cold War—the German Democratic Republic. In the minds of these inexperienced young people it evidently referred to a system in which a tiny group such as themselves could wield power for the American people but without having been elected by them. The justification for this highly undemocratic program was apparently that they knew what was good for the American people even if those people themselves did not. In other words, this would not really be a democracy, but rather a dictatorship of the enlightened, as they imagined themselves to be.

The statement went on to admit a difficulty: "we are a minority." That is of course a problem only in the context of a genuine democracy, but the inconsistency appears to have escaped the writers. And yet even this use of the word "minority" grossly inflated their own importance. A minority sounds like something that would constitute some reasonable percentage of the population, but at this time the SDS was a tiny fraction of one percent—about .0001 of one percent, to be more precise, or just a few hundred souls. For such a group to characterize what it and nobody else wanted as "democratic" was bizarre.

How then were they to acquire the power that they wanted? The answer was given in the last section of their statement, which was entitled "The University and Social Change." They would attain political power by taking over the universities:

An alliance of students and faculty…must wrest control of the
educational process from the administrative bureaucracy.…They
must import major public issues into the curriculum—research and
teaching on problems of war and peace is an outstanding example.…They must consciously build a base for their assault upon the
loci of power.

Why did they choose the universities as their path to political power?
Because "The university is located in a permanent position of social
influence. Its educational function makes it indispensable and automatically makes it a crucial institution in the formation of social attitudes."
These sentences are full of evasive circumlocutions, but what the writers
were really saying is that they wanted to use the universities preemptively to mold the attitudes of people even younger and more inexperienced
than themselves. There is a rather unkind word for this: indoctrination.
But given that their intent was obviously to shape opinion before young
students were able to gain sufficient experience and maturity to think
for themselves, that word is accurate enough. And so a tiny group of
extreme leftists decided that though they could never win at the ballot
box, they could still get what they wanted by gaining control over the
universities—which they eventually did.

We should be clear about the nature of what they were suggest-
ing. They were planning not to advance democracy but to subvert it.
Converting the universities into agencies for political control of the
general population is something done invariably by brutal dictatorships,
but never by liberal democracies. This is one of the most characteristic
differences between the two. SDS wanted us to believe that this was
democratic, but in fact it was advocating a giant step backward in our
political development as a nation: a reversion to the political mores of a
banana republic. Morally, the SDS program was a thoroughly disgraceful one. It envisaged a use of the universities that was both illegal and
unethical.

At this time, the common opinion among those who worked and
taught in academia was that such a program would destroy higher
education—and they had very good reasons to think so. But nobody
took SDS or its plan very seriously. The numbers of SDS radicals were

vanishingly small, and the ideas they wanted to promote were becoming discredited by the misery they produced wherever they were tried. How could the radicals possibly hope to succeed, and how could they in fact have succeeded in their plans for academia?

The answer is that they had one stroke of good fortune after another. A series of events now occurred each of which by itself greatly boosted their chances of success, and together they worked a miracle. The combination acted as a force multiplier, making it possible for the airy hopes of a handful of unrealistic malcontents to actually come to fruition.

• • •

The first of these historical contingencies was the national unrest over the mishandling of the war in Vietnam by the political class. The second was the sudden massive expansion of the universities at exactly the right, or rather, the wrong time—1965 to 1975. The third was the morphing of the civil rights movement into a powerful regime of identity politics marching under the banner of "diversity." Let's take these one by one.

Fifty years later, opinions still differ about whether the war in Vietnam had to be fought, and about the competence or incompetence of those who were in command of it. But what is beyond any doubt is that most young people at this time had the strong impression that both the generals and the politicians who authorized military action were incompetent and inhumane, and that tens of thousands on both sides were dying needlessly. The military draft inevitably made young adults feel more strongly about the matter than anyone else, and that brought about a strong anti-establishment atmosphere on the campuses. Both political parties were blamed for a policy that was widely thought of as cruel and corrupt—as well as highly dangerous to the health of those who might be drafted. Students felt that the government was covering up its failures by lying to the public about what was happening. Rightly or wrongly, the pervasive campus mood of this particular historical moment was much closer than usual to the habitual mindset of the radical left, which always tended to see conspiracies of the rich and powerful against ordinary people. As a result, membership in the SDS grew so rapidly that by 1968–69 it was two hundred times what it had been in 1962. If we assume (as we surely must) that the number who actually joined SDS was only a fraction of the total number of students who by now had a jaundiced attitude to the politicians who had produced this apparent mess, the general radicalization of political attitudes on campus must have been broader still.

And yet this mood would likely have died down in a few years without leaving behind much in the way of permanent damage to the campuses, had not a completely unrelated major historical event happened at exactly the same time. It was just at this moment that a massive expansion of higher education began. The confluence of these two historical events—the Vietnam War with its effect on the campus mood, and the dramatic growth of higher education—turned out to be astonishingly good luck for the radicals. By the same token, it was horrendously bad luck for the universities.

That second event had its roots in an earlier war. The end of World War II had meant a lot of catching up in lives whose normal course had been interrupted. People returned from military service to take up their ordinary lives again, and governments went back to projects that had necessarily been neglected. Children born to returning soldiers resulted in the "baby boom," which would greatly increase the demand for higher education during the 1960s. At the same time, the growing affluence of the population also led to more interest in college education. The numbers of students attending college rose steeply, beginning in the 1960s.

State governments saw the baby boomers approaching college age and began to build new campuses at an unprecedented rate. The nation's foremost and largest state university system, the University of California, created a whole series of new general campuses. Until the 1950s there had been only two, one in Berkeley and the other in Los Angeles. But in the period from 1958 to 1965, six more general campuses were founded, at Santa Barbara, Davis, Riverside, San Diego, Santa Cruz, and Irvine. This growth from two to eight general campuses in less than a decade was an extraordinary rate of expansion, and in retrospect highly dangerous.

As the boomers started to arrive on campus in the mid-Sixties, the total number of college students rose at a pace that was truly spectacular.

In 1965 there were 3.97 million college students at American public institutions, but by 1975 that figure had more than doubled, to 8.83 million. Private universities had a much smaller rate of expansion, but they account for a much smaller proportion of the total student numbers in higher education.

The sudden demand for huge numbers of new university and college teachers placed a great strain on the system. If student numbers suddenly more than doubled, then faculty numbers would have to grow by the same proportion. Therein lay an extremely serious problem. The quality of college faculty had always been kept up by the fact that only small numbers of new faculty jobs became available at any one time. Since the life of a university professor is an enviable one, the competition for each available opening was always fierce. Extraordinarily stiff competition kept quality up. But in the Sixties that normal situation changed out of all recognition. Newly founded universities and rapidly expanding older ones created a demand for new faculty appointments on a scale that had never been seen before. If professorial numbers were to keep pace with the increased student numbers of this decade, the number of new faculty appointments that were now needed was *greater than the number of all the existing professors in the nation.*

Even at the best of times, this sudden immensely increased demand would inevitably have meant a drastic lowering of quality. But this was a very long way from being the best of times: in fact, it was the worst time imaginable for recruiting new faculty on such a massive scale. The beginning of the frantic buildup of faculty and student numbers coincided almost exactly with the rise of serious domestic political unrest over the Vietnam War, and the resulting radicalization of a great many undergraduates and graduate students. The political turmoil and the unusual degree of radicalization on campus brought about by an increasingly unpopular war naturally had its greatest effect on those of draft age, which was precisely the group from which the huge expansion in college faculty numbers would have to come.

It would be hard to imagine a scenario better suited to advance the radical left's plan to control higher education. At exactly the moment when so many graduate students had been radicalized by political unrest over the Vietnam War, there was a desperate and unprecedented demand for them as new faculty members. As a consequence, the universities rapidly diluted their genuine, tried-and-tested academic teachers with large numbers of young people of a radical political mindset. This coincidence set in motion a shift from the 45 to 27 left/right ratio among faculty in 1969 to the virtual shutout of one side that we see today.

It's true that a university expansion on such a vast scale would have been hazardous at any time, as it would require a much less selective hiring process. At their best, university professors are so devoted to the pursuit of truth in their chosen fields that they are strongly resistant to corruption by political influence. That is the case with the genuinely original thinkers, and if they are a sufficiently large segment of the total faculty at a university, their values will predominate. But a huge expansion of faculty numbers will dilute the influence of the outstanding original thinkers. It will bring in many less able people who are not confident of their place in the fiercely competitive world of the university, and therefore more likely to be susceptible to fashionable attitudes and political currents. This danger was greatly magnified when the exceptionally large incoming faculty cohort included so many who were already heavily invested in radical politics.

One of the most puzzling aspects of the transformation of the universities over the last half century is the way in which the robust professional ethic of academic life could have been so completely overcome and swept aside. Only the frantic pace of the university expansion of 1965–1975 can explain what happened. Had Vietnam-era professorial appointments been made in the small numbers typical of other times, the appointees would have had to adapt to the entrenched professional ethic, or perish. But like the invading armies on D-Day, they arrived in numbers large enough to create a beachhead that quickly became so much a part of campus life that it could not be dislodged. This large contingent then seized on further opportunities to grow itself even more—and as we'll now see, major new opportunities did indeed soon arise. Moreover, these large numbers began to follow the logic that we saw in the last chapter: the greater the concentration of any political group, the more extreme it will become. Thus the political left on campus has grown more radical over time.

What do we mean when we call people political radicals? What makes them qualitatively different from mere left-leaners? First, for radicals, politics is everything, and everything is political. Pursuit of their political goals takes precedence over all else. The question of abusing and damaging universities for political purposes simply does not arise, since their political aims are so central for them that anything and everything must be used in order to achieve them. There can be no troubled conscience about misusing whatever might help to get them where they want to be politically. The second defining characteristic of radicals is that they have no interest in debate, as their minds are already made up. The goal is obvious to them, and so submitting it to discussion simply wastes time and energy. Only one thing matters: action to implement the plan. Third, the goal is nothing less than a deep transformation of society. Radicals might differ among themselves as to exactly what that transformation will consist in, but they all agree that it must be thoroughgoing. Nothing else really matters to them—certainly not the integrity of universities. This means that political radicals are the very last people we should ever want to have running our universities: their values are the reverse of academic values. Yet they now control academia.

Meanwhile, a third historical event served to engender something even more damaging to the integrity of universities: identity politics and the gradual adoption of "diversity" as their guiding light, one that soon replaced their traditional and proper concern with intellectual excellence. Here was yet another opportunity for faculty radicals to swell their own numbers on campus.

The idea of "diversity" as the ruling doctrine in academia grew out of a genuinely positive step forward, the Civil Rights Act of 1964. At last, there was a legal guarantee that discrimination by reason of race must end, and that people would henceforth be treated on their merits as individuals. No longer could black students be barred from campuses because of race; now they would be admitted on the same standards as anyone else, based on their fitness to undertake the course of study and their ability to compete successfully with the other students. All were to be judged on individual merit. But it quickly became obvious that some colleges were ignoring the plain language of the Civil Rights Act and abandoning merit-based criteria in admissions so that they could still use race as a factor, but now in order to increase the numbers of black students.

This might seem at first sight to be something of no great importance for the overall functioning of universities, since all that was involved was admitting a few more black students than might otherwise have been the case. But in fact something far more important and dangerous was happening: identity politics was being inserted into the life of the campuses. Institutions whose very nature requires them to judge ideas only by their intellectual coherence, and people only by their abilities, were being asked to introduce an alien element into their culture, one plainly inconsistent with it. Moreover it was one that contained no self-limiting principle. If bending the rules a little for a few students was now to be considered acceptable, why would it not be acceptable to bend them much more and for much greater numbers? Once it starts, there is no end to the operation of identity politics, which means that its ability to corrupt academia is limitless.

My own introduction to the way in which identity politics undermines honesty and decency was quite by chance. In 1963, I joined a university in western Canada as an assistant professor. As I arrived, a court case was in the headlines of the local newspaper day after day. A man who had been the city's mayor for many years was forced from office because he attempted to use that office to enrich himself by rezoning land that he himself owned. An inquiry found him unambiguously guilty of gross misconduct, and the city sued him. To settle the suit he had to pay the city $100,000, a huge sum in 1963. On the day he settled the suit I remarked to faculty friends that we were fortunate to be rid of this crooked mayor. One of those friends gave me a pitying look and told me that *of course* this man would run again for mayor in the fall, and he'd win without any trouble. I couldn't believe what I was hearing. Surely a man who had been found guilty of a serious fraud and abuse of office couldn't possibly win reelection? Oh yes, he could, came the reply; he's Ukrainian, and all of the Ukrainians in the city will block-vote for him regardless of what he has done. At that time, the sizable Ukrainian community was a large portion of the city's electorate, and no other candidate could win virtually 100 percent of the vote among so solid an electoral bloc. My friend turned out to be correct: the man did indeed run again for mayor and won easily.

I had not been exposed to that kind of identity-group politics when I was growing up in London immediately after World War II, before ethnic divisions had yet become a significant factor in politics there. In that environment, it was safe to say that known crooks could not win at the ballot box. It was a great shock to me to learn that all the values that should matter—honesty, integrity, managerial ability, and so on—could be swamped by tribal solidarity, which is another term for identity politics. Nothing in my life so far had prepared me for this. But that mayoral election should have been a guide to what could later happen in higher education in America when group identity was made into the highest value, rather than something that we should rise above in a modern society.

Senator Orrin Hatch pulled no punches when talking about identity politics in an opinion piece for the *Wall Street Journal*. He called it "a blight on our democracy" and "a cancer on our political culture." Identity politics is "tribalism by another name," wrote Hatch. "It is the deliberate and often unnatural segregation of people into categories for political gain." The senator declared that "Ideas, not identity, should be the driving force of our politics."[1]

Ideas, not identity, should even more be the driving force in our colleges and universities. But identity politics has taken over, and is one of the most important (possibly the most important) of the ways in which the radical left has cemented its control of the campuses. The effect on the American academy has been profoundly destructive.

• • •

To understand the magnitude of the damage that eventually resulted from a seemingly innocuous effort to admit a few more minority students, we need to look at how a policy of race-based admissions began to change the entire system of thought and behavior on college campuses. Bringing in a small number of students and faculty who might not otherwise have been admitted sounds like a circumscribed kind of thing that wouldn't affect anything else. But small changes can trigger other changes, which lead to still others, until a chain of reactions adds up to something that overwhelms the system.

The series of changes initiated by racial preferences in admissions began in the 1970s, as pressure grew for colleges and universities to admit more black students. That pressure increased in scope as well, with other minorities—chiefly Hispanics—added to the preferred list, so that the numbers of students involved escalated. Pressure to hire minority faculty also intensified, until every new faculty appointment was viewed as an opportunity to increase minority faculty numbers. Many departments began to do what was expected of them, especially in the humanities and social sciences. But as this happened, an unintended consequence of monumental importance began to appear: the political complexion of the faculty was being further altered. Here was yet another factor leading inexorably to radical dominance of the campuses.

It was inevitable that the people who were most enthusiastic about the need for racial preferences in faculty hiring were also the most influential in making the appointments. And just as inevitably, the kinds of people they looked for and appointed were those who shared in their enthusiasm. But that enthusiasm correlated with something else: a strong sense of the injustices of the past, and of the need to remake society. This meant that political radicals were in a position to seek out and hire more people who were just as radical as they were. Racial preferences in faculty hiring turned out to be yet another of the ways in which the number of radical leftists on campus was increased and the political complexion of the faculty was moved still more toward the radical left.

When potential new faculty appointees were being considered in the past, what always mattered most was intellectual curiosity and a capacity for developing new ideas. The quality that now came to the fore was not intellectual flexibility but its opposite: a determined and inflexible political commitment. Yet more people were added to the faculty who by temperament were not suited for academic life. Instead of teaching students how to sift evidence and weigh alternative explanations intelligently, the new faculty hires would promote the fixed mental framework of political radicals, which has no use for weighing alternatives.

The scope of preferential hiring was further enlarged in an effort to add more women to the faculty. Here again, those who were most vocal about the need for more female faculty members were most influential in the hiring process, and they tended to seek out women who shared their own burning sense that the status quo was unjust and that social change was needed. Even more faculty were being added who didn't have the academic's habit of examining and evaluating ideas and evidence, but instead the political zealot's firmly fixed attitudes about radical social change. Intellectual inflexibility, not curiosity, was their most prominent attribute. The anti-academic segment of the faculty was growing stronger and stronger.

Identity politics was also helped along by a persistent weakness of college humanities departments: their vulnerability to fads and fashions. The reason for this weakness is that scholars need to say something new about their subject, but novelty doesn't come so naturally in the study of English literature, for example, as it does in physics or biochemistry. Most discoveries in the sciences open up other areas for investigation. That was the case in the early 1950s when a number of researchers were trying to discover the structure of DNA, and many of them certainly felt thwarted when Francis Crick and James Watson beat them to it, but their consolation was that the discovery immediately opened up vast new areas for research. By contrast, a groundbreaking book on Shakespeare rarely does the same for competing Shakespeare scholars. On the contrary, it just makes it harder for them to find anything new to say about the subject.

That is where fads and fashions in literary criticism come in. A new vogue for, say, a psychological approach to Shakespeare provides a way of introducing novelty, though an artificial and poorly grounded one. New fads and fashions in criticism are a way in which people who have no real originality of thought can find something new to say—or at least appear to do so.

The campus obsession with race and gender seemed to offer a new approach to literary criticism. And so the growing tide of campus radicalism got substantial support from faculty who were not themselves politically motivated but jumped on the race-and-gender bandwagon as a career vehicle. By the time those people realized what was really happening, their departments had already been taken over by people who were not merely playing academic games but were really serious about their politicized scholarship. In the humanities especially, the rule of fads and fashion was another factor that helped the radical left gain control.

Still more dominos were to fall, and more unintended consequences appeared.

While established college departments were increasingly influenced by radical politics, there was still a sense that they were governed by the traditional academic values of analysis and inquiry. And so they were bound to be constraining for people who have no interest in those values. Faculty radicals who had been appointed in order to achieve race and gender diversity soon pressed for new departments of their own, where they would make their own rules. New departments of Women's Studies, Black Studies, Ethnic Studies and the like soon arose.[2] Such departments were inconceivable before the era of race- and gender-based admissions and hiring preferences.

In the early Seventies, the idea of a separate Black Studies department was generally rejected wherever it was suggested. The spirit of that time called for integration, not segregation, and everyone recognized that black history or women's history was first and foremost history: it needed a historian's skills and could only be evaluated by a historian's standards in an environment of other historians. For academics, the historian's methodology was basic, and the particular topic incidental. But for political radicals, the reverse was true. So the new departments were in effect a series of little anti-academies within the academy, places where unacademic thought and behavior could thrive. The typical voice in those departments was not the careful, analytical speech of academic life, but instead the strident, carelessly expressed and poorly supported conspiracy theories of street politics. The University of Colorado's infamous Ward Churchill (discussed in Chapter Seven) was not an isolated case but typical of these new departments. Naturally, new departments needed more professors to staff them, which meant still more political radicals added to the faculty, and still greater campus influence for radicalism.

But even given all the powerful factors that boosted the numbers of radicals on campus—the Vietnam War, the huge expansion of higher education, the large-scale recruitment of political radicals under the cover of increasing the minority and female presence on campus—one might still wonder how a group that was so diametrically opposed to genuine academic values could have prospered in an environment that had formerly been so completely devoted to those values. The answer is something of a paradox: they were successful precisely *because* they were so out of step with the values of the academy that administrations and faculty alike were completely unprepared to deal with them. Serious academic scholars are used to going their own individual way, whether in pursuit of a research program that they define for themselves or in a classroom where they alone set the agenda. Organizing them is like herding cats. But political radicals knew very well how to organize themselves for a common goal, and how to create pressures that academics were not used to dealing with. In the academic world, reason and analysis had always been the most powerful weapons in any dispute, but that was only because everyone on campus had agreed that they were. When a group suddenly appeared among them that refused to respect the supremacy of reasoned argument and instead used the political means of demonstrations, disruptions, and moral blackmail, ordinary academics were helpless. Their trusted weapons seemed like bows and arrows in the age of tank warfare.

• • •

Another major boost to the power of political radicalism on campus came with a court decision in 1978. It was the case of Alan Bakke, a white man who had been refused admission to the medical school of the University of California at Davis, although his credentials were superior to those of some minority students who were admitted. Bakke sued, and his case went all the way to the U.S. Supreme Court. In a strange decision, four justices ruled unambiguously that race was an inadmissible factor in college admissions, while another four said that it was perfectly acceptable when used to remedy past injustices. The swing vote was that of Justice Lewis Powell, who joined each side in one respect, but issued a one-man decision that in combination with parts of the two opposing opinions became the law of the land. Powell outlawed racial quotas as an unconstitutional use of race in admissions, but in a fateful turn of phrase he ruled that seeking diversity in the student body was a legitimate and lawful goal.

Powell thought he had given permission for just a modest amount of admitting by race while outlawing overt large-scale quotas, but in fact his ruling did something entirely different. University administrations immediately took Powell's opinion to be all the justification they needed for de facto racial quotas. But it took somewhat longer for a much more dangerous consequence of Powell's ruling to emerge. While the argument over college admissions was conducted using the language of racial quotas and preferences, the pro-quota side was at a disadvantage: those words were unpopular and obviously clashed with the language of the Constitution. But Powell had unwittingly made it possible to replace them with an attractive concept that was to become much more than a convenient euphemism: it came to serve as the proud banner for what could now be portrayed as a noble crusade. Powell's use of the concept of "diversity" allowed identity politics to seize the moral high ground on campus.

"Diversity" soon became the key value in academic life; the campus obsession with it developed into a mania that swept common sense aside. Administrators could wrap themselves in it and acquire invulnerability, no small thing for people who had always had brickbats thrown at them by faculty and students with great regularity. By championing diversity they were automatically on the side of the angels. Campus radicals benefited enormously from this change of language: their efforts were central to diversity, and so they moved from the periphery to the center of the campus. In any confrontation, opposition to the radicals, and so to diversity, could easily be stigmatized as moral failure, a mean-spirited refusal to join the great crusade.

The importance of "diversity" in weakening resistance to radical control of the campuses would be difficult to overstate. It gave a whole new focus to midlevel administrators—department chairs, deans, provosts, vice presidents. They had always been the quality control of higher education; their job was to monitor the integrity of academic life. If you were to examine any speech made by a university president fifty years ago, you would find that the word "excellence" occurs with great frequency. That concept was the guiding light of the academy. If you made the same examination now, you'd find that "diversity" has taken its place. Senior administrators of the old school learned that if they ever acted as their old watchword "excellence" required them to, the result would be an ugly fight with the rising radical powers on campus. So they were content to have a new banner to wave, one that would not get them into any trouble. And when the most recently appointed administrators had gotten their jobs only after the radicals had approved them, they found "diversity" a splendid flag to sail under.

So potent was this concept that a new type of administrative office devoted to it began to appear. Typically, these offices would have titles that contained the words "diversity" or "inclusion" or "equity," or all three. They sprang up at all levels of campus administration, from the departmental level all the way up to the president's office. The new bureaucrats appointed to staff these offices were not shy about asserting their will. Midlevel administrators had always been careful not to offend the faculty because the latter outranked them in the campus pecking order, but these new administrators knew that having the word "diversity" in their title allowed them to throw their weight about. When Christina Hoff Sommers was shouted down at Lewis and Clark College (as discussed in Chapter One), it was one of these midlevel diversity administrators who took it upon herself to order Sommers to wrap up her lecture immediately. It is highly doubtful whether she really had the authority to do this, but nobody wanted to question whether she did.

The combined total of funds spent to set up and staff "diversity" offices is enormous. When a new vice chancellorship for diversity and inclusion is invented, the appointee is given a very generous salary (at least $200,000) and commensurate support staff. But this new office would only add to large numbers of existing offices already dealing with diversity. In her book *The Diversity Delusion*, Heather Mac Donald lists all the diversity offices on the UC San Diego campus, and the list goes on for half a page.[3] These offices greatly increased the number of radical activists on campus and gave the radicals powerful support from the campus bureaucracy.[4]

Several years before Justice Powell's decision launched the doctrine of "diversity" and a plethora of campus bureaucrats, a provision of the Education Amendments of 1972 had given rise to another set of offices that quickly expanded far beyond their original scope and purpose. The new Title IX offices on campuses around the country were intended to make sure that female student athletes had as much access to sports funding as male athletes, but they soon became ruthless enforcers of radical campus ideology with respect to any aspect of relations between males and females. Christina Hoff Sommers gives a picture of what this bureaucracy is doing:

> Schools have now developed elaborate "sex bureaucracies" to educate, monitor, train, investigate, and punish. Harvard has fifty full- and part-time Title IX coordinators. Yale has thirty. Swarthmore College—with only 1,500 students—has a network of Title IX deputy coordinators, fellows, investigators, and advisers. On campuses throughout the country, students and faculty are now routinely denied due-process rights. Hundreds of students, mostly young men, have been subject to kangaroo courts and expelled from school.[5]

It is safe to say that the enormous increase in the size of campus administration in the last few decades is due to the creation of these ubiquitous diversity offices more than to anything else. Students rightly complain about tuition increases that have far outstripped inflation in recent years, but the clamor by student activists for more diversity administrators is the most important part of the cost problem that they complain of. Whenever any kind of campus incident offends either minority or female students or both, it has become commonplace for students to include in their list of nonnegotiable demands the appointment of some new diversity office or other that will become yet one more enforcer of the radical ideology of campus political activists. It never seems to occur to them that their skyrocketing tuition pays for these unproductive diversity bureaucrats that they keep demanding more of.

The startling growth in diversity offices has changed the relation of faculty to administration. Power had always been jealously guarded by the faculty, but these new bureaucracies flex their muscles as none before. As George Leef has said, these new diversity offices "usually attract social justice warrior types who are eager to impose their values on everyone else"[6] Writing in the *Wall Street Journal*, Philip Hamburger put the matter even more strongly: they promote "indoctrination and censorious intrusions into speech, opinion and personal life."[7] They are now a crucial part of the way in which political radicals exercise power on campus, and in which identity politics now strangles academia.

These new offices are also a classic example of perverse incentives. The extent of their power on campus is inversely proportional to their success in their ostensible mission. With no racial or sexual tensions on campus they would shrink into unimportance, since they would have nothing to do. But their importance grows amid race- or gender-based strife, and so Title IX officers in particular have a stake in padding their caseloads as much as possible. Other governmental offices devoted to policing crime have a vested interest in seeing crime rates lower—they can then take credit for less crime. But an office devoted to sexual harassment has the opposite incentive: the more sexual harassment there is, the more the office is needed, and the more it can grow and throw its weight around. This is indeed a perverse incentive—an incentive to find or invent and then magnify as much trouble as possible. In effect, these poisonous offices have a stake in creating racial and sexual divisions so that they themselves will be needed to respond to them.

A case from my own campus (UC Santa Cruz) illustrates how this works in practice. Until quite recently, the Title IX office had a staff of only one. Then, within a period of three years, that individual increased the size of her office to five investigators plus support personnel—an astonishing percentage increase in so short a time. Naturally, her reported caseload skyrocketed, though nobody had noticed any corresponding changes in the behavior of men and women on campus. Just how and why the office's caseload soared can be seen in the following incident.

A distinguished scholar who was head of a large laboratory was talking to his female secretary. She mentioned self-deprecatingly that her sister was much prettier than she herself. Her boss didn't want to leave her with the impression that he agreed with her negative self-evaluation, so he said encouragingly that of course she was pretty too. A man who had just been turned down for a teaching job in the department overheard this casual remark and retaliated by submitting a complaint that the professor had sexually harassed his secretary. Though the secretary herself said that this was just silly, and that she had in no way either felt or been sexually harassed, the Title IX coordinator went ahead with a full-scale investigation, which she kept going for many months. Faced with a situation that was so plainly irrational, the professor thought he had better hire a lawyer to defend himself. Perhaps the lawyer scared the Title IX coordinator, because she soon dropped the matter, but not until hundreds of hours had been diverted from the professor's research and students, to say nothing of many thousands of dollars in legal fees. This completely spurious case increased the coordinator's caseload numbers, and its only real point seems to have been to bolster the case for more staff. More staff supervised is the road to higher status and pay for any office head. Senior administrators ought to be on the alert for potential self-aggrandizement in such cases—except that they too seem to like the larger case numbers that support the radical narrative of rampant sexism and racism on campus.

The change from a focus on excellence to one on diversity has also altered the pecking order within the faculty. The arbiters of excellence, those who defined it and judged it on any campus, had been those members of the faculty who had earned international prominence in their fields. They were the natural campus leaders because they most embodied the core values of the academy: original thought and intellectual curiosity. Administrators always knew that they were mainly answerable to this group of distinguished senior faculty, and appointments to the administration were often made from its ranks. But when diversity edged out excellence as the leading concept on campus, all of that changed. The arbiters of diversity were not the intellectual giants of the campus, but instead the political radicals—the intellectual mediocrities. They were the ones who now led the way and could demand that their judgments be the basis of policy. Administrators formerly needed to maintain the confidence of their most accomplished faculty, but now they were desperate to keep the diversity lobby happy instead. Faculty leadership had passed from those most committed to the academy's core values to those who least embodied them.

. . .

So far we've looked at the major factors that allowed political radicalism on campus to grow and to flourish, but what of the watchdog mechanisms that were supposed to keep the campuses intellectually healthy and prevent their becoming politicized? In theory there were three levels of oversight mechanisms that should have stopped the rot: faculty committees whose job it was to monitor both the quality of new faculty appointees and the overall integrity of academic life; midlevel administrators whose job it was to enforce quality control in their departments; and boards of trustees or regents, who were there to represent the public interest in higher education. All of them failed miserably, though for different reasons.

As we've seen, the replacement of "excellence" by "diversity" crippled administrative quality control. Candidates for administrative office were now routinely asked the key question in any interview: What would you do for diversity if you were appointed? It was soon apparent that any candidate for an administrative post who did not pronounce diversity to be his or her highest priority could not be appointed. Public opposition by the campus diversity lobby would be fatal. Everyone now knew that any sign of independent thinking about diversity would mean the end of an administrative career. Thus began a generation of weak administrators who were either easily intimidated by the radicals to whom they owed their jobs, or else themselves fully committed to diversity and all that it entailed, including radicalism. Either way, administrative quality control was effectively put out of action.

Faculty watchdog committees failed for the very simple reason that they became radicalized as the faculty became radicalized. It soon became obvious that it was pointless to appeal to them. An instructive example occurred on the UC Santa Cruz campus. A faculty political lobby that called itself "Faculty Against the War" organized a "teach-in" against the Iraq war. The group claimed that their event would be an educational one, and so asked for university funds to support the event. A genuinely educational event would have had speakers for and against, at a minimum offering an initial explanation of the stated rationale for the war, and the case against. The aim would be to promote understanding of what had happened and why. But of the ten speakers for this event, every one was virulently antiwar. The roster of speakers made it crystal clear that the intent was not to promote understanding, but instead to promote opposition to the war—a political motive, not an educational one. To call it a teach-in was fraudulent.

Nevertheless, the event received funding from the offices of the chancellor and of the executive vice chancellor, as well as from five colleges, nine departments, and four research units, which added up to a great deal of public money. A member of the campus faculty decided to question whether support of what was clearly a political rally rather than an educational event was a proper use of university funds, and she brought the matter to the faculty senate's Committee on Academic Freedom. But the chair of that committee was the main organizer of the event! She was Bettina Aptheker, a women's studies professor and daughter of the well-known American Communist leader Herbert Aptheker. In the "by any means necessary" spirit of political radicals everywhere, Aptheker refused to recuse herself in spite of the most blatant conflict of interest, and used her position as chair to prevent discussion of the matter. Not a single committee member intervened to insist that recusal in such circumstances was automatic, yet it was undeniable that Aptheker could not be both the subject of the committee's inquiry and the leader of that inquiry. The committee's faculty radicals didn't care about the flagrant conflict: they had complete control of the committee, and for them that was all there was to it. So much for faculty watchdog committees.

In this way, faculty quality control mechanisms at all levels became worthless as soon as political activists were numerous enough to control them. But that still left governing boards that were usually composed of members of the public who were independent of the campuses. Those boards usually have charters that give them the task of acting on behalf of the public to maintain the integrity of a university. The most important responsibility assigned to them is to keep their institutions free of political corruption. In the case of the University of California, for example, the state's constitution gives the Board of Regents an explicit last-resort responsibility, one that the Regents themselves repeat in their 1970 policy statement on academic freedom: "[The Regents] are responsible to see that the University remain aloof from politics and never function as an instrument for the advance of partisan interest. Misuse of the classroom by, for example, allowing it to be used for political indoctrination . . . constitutes misuse of the University as an institution."

How have governing boards done in carrying out their charge? The one thing that can be said with absolute certainty is that as last-resort watchdogs they have been completely useless. Why that has been so is a complex question, but the fact of it is not. They have stood by and done nothing as higher education declined precipitously. They have been the most toothless watchdogs of all. When in 2012 the California Association of Scholars (CAS) presented a report to the UC Board of Regents that set out in considerable detail all the ways in which the University of California was being corrupted by radical politics, the chair of the board, Sherry Lansing, simply refused to put it on the agenda. (The report and its reception are discussed in Chapter Seven.)

Why have regents and trustees been so lazy and irresponsible, here in California and elsewhere? Each local situation may be different, but a general unwillingness on the part of regents and trustees to make waves is unmistakable. It has frequently been said that campus administrations exercise iron control over what a governing board is allowed to see, but that can't be the whole answer. To judge from the situation in California, one answer at least is this: a seat on the University of California's Board of Regents has great social prestige. A regent will rub shoulders not only with the president of a world-famous university, but also with California's governor and lieutenant governor. Few regents have any expert knowledge of higher education, and some have only minimal educational credentials. The Wikipedia article on the Regents of the University of California candidly says that "The vast majority of the Regents appointed by the Governor historically have consisted of lawyers, politicians and businessmen." Many are the kind of businessmen or women who have built a large business from scratch and become wealthy as a result. They typically contribute financially both to the university and to the appointing governor's campaign, but are often intimidated by major figures in the academic world. Most enjoy the prestige of their appointment far too much to cause any trouble. And it generally does not go well for them if they do, as the former regent John Moores found out.

Moores was a highly accomplished man. Unlike most regents, he had a doctoral degree, and he had also had two quite different careers, both very successful—the first in computer software, the second in sports. In 1994 he had become the owner of the San Diego Padres, and in 1999 a regent of the University of California. He was also a trustee and later chair of the former U.S. president's Carter Center. Moores was one of the best-qualified regents ever to have served on the board, and so he quickly became its chair. He took his UC oversight responsibility seriously, and that soon got him into trouble.

When the question of racial preferences in admissions came up, Moores understandably wanted to make sure that he and the other regents had all the relevant facts at their fingertips so that they could make a well-informed decision. He investigated the average test scores of undergraduate minority admittees in relation to overall average scores, not realizing ahead of time just how toxic that issue was. What he found was that the discrepancy in test scores between minority students and the rest was much greater than anyone imagined. Moores assumed that regents would want to know exactly what they were doing, and so he told them the facts. He was taken completely by surprise when he was viciously attacked by faculty, administration, and many regents, all of whom didn't want those facts to become public. Probably at the instigation of UC's administration, the board passed a motion censuring Moores. He soon left the board in disgust, and his trenchant judgment of the usefulness of the regents has become a thing of legend: they are "about as relevant as furniture when it comes to governing." Moores is not alone here. Two other former regents, Fabian Nunez and Ward Connerly, have also criticized UC's expectation that regents will never make waves.

What happened to John Moores was a warning to regents and trustees everywhere: if you do your job conscientiously where campus politicization is concerned, you will be vilified. The public gave these boards the ultimate responsibility and the power to protect the integrity of the universities, but experience teaches us that they will never lift a finger to do so.

In this chapter I've tried to answer the question how the catastrophic corruption of colleges and universities was able to happen. In the next two chapters I'll turn to the damage that these corrupted institutions are now doing to education and more generally to the entire fabric of the nation.

CHAPTER 4

Sabotaging Education
for Citizenship

In the past, higher education has always included a grounding in the accumulated knowledge and wisdom of our society and of the civilization of which it is a part: its history, institutions, constitutional framework, literature, and scientific knowledge. Each individual student might choose a program of study that emphasized one or two of these subject areas more than others, but almost everyone would get at least some grounding in all of them. Exposure to knowledge of their society's origins, achievements, and thought made students broadly educated people who as a consequence could be more productive members of that society. But education for citizenship is no longer happening on college campuses, and what takes its place is far worse than nothing, because much of what students are taught is doing more harm than good.

Arguably the most important part of an education for citizenship in the United States is providing students with a realistic and honest account of their country's history. Everyone should know how the country developed, and the key stages in how we got to the point we are now at. What have been our successes and failures—what has worked, and what didn't? What has been well done, and what should have been done differently? How did the problems we face now come into being? What in our history goes on the same lines as what other countries have done, and what is unique to us?

But American history as now taught on college campuses is largely distorted and risible. Why this is so follows inexorably from what is always the first concern of political radicals: to make the case for radical social change. To make the case for change that will be drastic and far-reaching, they must paint as dark a picture of America as possible, for only if people are persuaded that something is completely rotten will they accept that it needs to be transformed into something very different. There are two main ways in which the radicals seek to do this. The first consists in looking only at those aspects of American history that speak to its failings—some real, but many imagined—while carefully avoiding the nation's many positive accomplishments. The second consists in ignoring the fact that the way people think about and treat each other has greatly changed for the better during the last two hundred years, as the influence of the Enlightenment values developed by northern Europeans and their North American offshoot spread far and wide. Radicals routinely use decidedly modern standards of behavior to find fault with the very people who during earlier times led the way in the development of those standards. Let's take these points one by one.

First, radicals attempt to blacken their country by the cherry-picking of negatives in American history. In so doing, they falsify history and evade obvious questions that even the most superficial acquaintance with the country ought to suggest. For example, it is a simply amazing fact that the United States grew from a few fairly insignificant colonies on the eastern coast of the American continent to being by far the most powerful nation on earth, militarily, economically, and culturally, in only two hundred years, though its population was never more than one-third of that of India or China. Any genuine historical scholar would have his or her intellectual curiosity immediately engaged by something so striking that it cries out for an explanation, but this is of no interest to radical activists. In fact, it's a very great nuisance for them, because it would require them to acknowledge that America has been a successful country in these respects. American successes lessen the case for radical social change, and for that reason they are passed over. American failures are what radicals need either to find or to invent. That is why their history of America is so heavily distorted.

But this astonishing transformation in such a short time is only the beginning of a long list of unique factors in American history. Add to this that its citizens have just about the highest standard of living in the world; that it is the oldest democracy in the world, with the longest-surviving written constitution; and that America was preeminent in the development of modernity itself—the way that people all over the globe now live. American technology and industrial methods have helped to spread a sharp rise in living standards across the globe. Aviation was invented in America, and it has made the world a much smaller place. Lifespans have doubled across the globe due to modern medicine, which America had a significant role in developing. But it was not only in material respects that America led the way in the development of modernity. After the Second World War, America restored or installed democracy in both its vanquished Axis foes and countries it liberated, which still enjoy and thrive under it—while the Soviet Union enslaved the countries it "liberated" and made them part of its empire.

An honest and realistic history of America could not fail to deal with its extraordinarily rapid rise to the status of the most culturally influential country on earth, with the strongest economy and the most powerful military. It would also have to note that no militarily supreme power has ever been so restrained; its predecessors going all the way back to the Romans have never failed to pursue conquest to the limit of their ability. But American history as written by campus radicals ignores all these salient features of American history. In place of these glaringly obvious facts about the unique status of America in the modern world, it generally gives us narrowly focused, small-scale, blinkered accounts, designed only to afford opportunities to carp at America's mean-spiritedness and failures.

We can get a sense of what is happening to the study of American history if we look at the roster of the American history courses on offer in a particular session on an American campus. I'll give a few examples, chosen at random; almost any campus would show the same kind of result.

The main bulk of coursework in a history department lies in its collection of upper-division courses for a given session. On the UC Santa Barbara campus in the fall term of 2018, there were eight upper-division courses in American history. Identity politics, with its habitual focus on grievance rather than knowledge, was prominent in most of them.

There was History 159B: Women in American History, where according to the course description, attention would be given to "racial, class and ethnic differences," as well as feminist thought. History 168B: History of the Chicanos would trace "the social-cultural lifeline of the Mexicans [!] who have lived north of Mexico," while History 179A: Native American History to 1838, was yet another identity-group course. History 161B: Colonial and Revolutionary America, might seem to have a more general focus, but the course description soon made it clear that this too was going to be about identity politics, with an emphasis on "the interaction of Native Americans, Europeans, and African Americans." The same would be true of History 164B: American Immigration, which would concern itself with "enduring racial and ethnic hierarchies." History 175B: American Cultural History at first appeared to be more general, but again the description announced the same focus on identity politics, specifically on "dominant and alternative representations of American values and identity." As always, identity politics means above all else a focus on grievance.

None of these courses offers a general sense of the nation's history or any mention of its unique successes. Instead, they all look at specific groups and themes no doubt chosen for their potential for carping and for condemnation of the United States. There would be much about the injustices committed by the powerful against the powerless: minorities, immigrants, and women. Four of the courses pick specific targets of oppression, but the others make it clear that they too will focus on oppression of those groups. The result is that in the upper-division American history courses of that session at UC Santa Barbara there was almost no trace of anything that has made America such a successful and highly influential country, and nothing that illustrated its leading role in the development of modern life. Anyone who knew only the content of this particular roster of courses would form a general impression of an evil and dysfunctional country.

Let's move on randomly to another time and place: the UC San Diego campus's fall 2010 upper-division courses in American history. Yet again, there were courses that offered the familiar opportunities to carp about America's mistreatment of various classes of its citizens, but nothing that gave a more general sense of what is distinctive about the nation's history. By its title, History 146: Race, Riots, and Violence in the U.S. leaves us in no doubt that victimology was at the core of the course. But it's actually worse than that. The course description reads: "Exploring how different groups of Americans have constructed competing notions of race, gender, labor, and national belonging by participating in street violence." Apparently, street violence is a justified and even heroic response to the injustices committed by American society.

History 139: African American History in the 20th Century is described as a course about "the transformation of African America" by "imperialism, migration, urbanization, desegregation, and deindustrialization." History 156: American Women/American Womanhood was about "a dominant ideology of womanhood…witchcraft, evangelicalism, cult of domesticity, sexuality, rise of industrial capitalism." History 180: Immigration and Ethnicity in American Society was also about oppression. Then there was History 154: Western Environmental History, which might sound less victim-obsessed, except that here too the course description begins with an emphasis on ethnicity, indicating that the same sort of attitudes would shape the presentation. The title of History 151: American Legal History might allow the hope that it could escape from the ever-present radical mindset, but the description dashes that hope: the course "examines race relations and law, the rise of big business, the origins of the modern welfare state during the Great Depression, the crisis of civil liberties produced by two world wars and McCarthyism."

These two examples of complete course rosters are typical of American campuses; the same result could be found almost anywhere. They are certainly typical of my own campus, UC Santa Cruz. Extreme negativism reigns, but that nagging question remains: Didn't America ever do anything right? How can it be that a country that has led the way in the development of modern life is the miserable place represented in these courses? How can so many want to come and live here if it is so bad? In fact, why is this the country that more people want to migrate to than any other on earth? These questions are never asked, but real historians would feel compelled to ask them.

Evidently, most instructors now choose these highly specific, narrowly defined topics in American history because they offer the most scope for their jaundiced views of the country. But in the much smaller number of cases where an instructor takes on the whole sweep of the nation's history—that is, in general surveys—the results are even more astounding.

The two examples I'll use to illustrate this are not random choices; they are in fact highly prominent ones. The first is a course that is taught in the large and important history department of one of the nation's greatest universities, the University of California at Berkeley. The course is central to that department's work, because it has the distinction of being the only course in America history that is required for the major program. Since the entire department determines the policy that makes it a required course, its content must be known and approved by every member of the history faculty. As such, it cannot possibly be regarded as an atypical course or one that is an unfortunate accident. It is History 7, which has two parts, A and B, one of which must be completed for a history major.

History 7A has the very general title: "The United States from Settlement to the Civil War." This suggests a general introduction without specific emphasis on one or another aspect of the country's historical development. Precisely for that reason, it's jarring to read the more detailed description of its content in an official printed catalog for the campus. The course will, according to this account, bring the student to "understand how democratic political institutions emerged in the United States in this period in the context of an economy that depended on slave labor and violent land acquisition." This must surely take us aback. Course descriptions traditionally spell out the scope of the course, and do not (and must not) prejudge whatever contentious issues may arise during the course of the class. But the Berkeley historian who composed this course description is so completely in the grip of an animus against his country that he blurts it out right away, recording it in the printed campus catalog, thus prejudging everything when he should instead have been giving a factual description of the ground to be covered. He cannot wait to tell his students that they must take it as a given that the U.S. Constitution is tainted by the fact that those who wrote it stole their land from Indians and were racist slaveowners. He is determined to get the attention of his students onto those facts first, to make sure that they don't start off with the usual (and from his point of view completely mistaken) admiration for the oldest functioning constitution in the world, and for the careful thought and knowledge that went into its composition. The instructor wants the students to think first of all that it was conceived by evil people. In effect, he smears the Constitution.

Evidently, this professor is someone with a very large axe to grind, someone intent on making his students adopt his own anger and contempt for his country and see it in the same jaundiced way that he sees it. A genuine academic scholar and teacher simply does not do this—he doesn't start off with rigid preemptive conclusions before the course material has even been looked at. But UC Berkeley's History 7A has been twisted into the shape of an alienated radical's indictment of his country before the teaching begins. A genuinely academic inquiry would have to look at many different aspects of the context in which the political institutions of the United States arose, and those would include at the very least the tradition of English political philosophy as well as English common law, and the experience of the colonists under colonial rule that led to the Revolutionary War. But the instructor was determined that exclusive prominence should be given to the sheer nastiness (as he sees it) of the Americans of the time, regardless of the logic of the constitution they wrote. Most observers have been deeply impressed with the depth of the founding fathers' understanding of political philosophy, and with the genius of the document they produced, but that traditional appraisal of the U.S. Constitution obviously annoys this instructor. He wants to cut those founding fathers down to size right at the outset: they were racists! For him, this is what is really important—not getting his students to understand the thought processes that went into the Constitution. He has no interest in a balanced account of the colonists' strengths and weaknesses, which is what academic analysis requires. His concerns are those of all radical political activists: he wants to make converts to his own political ideology. In a professor, that is thoroughly unprofessional behavior.

From the course description alone we could guess what happens in the History 7 classroom, but another published source tells us more directly. Between 2002 and 2011 the website noindoctrination.org documented cases of propagandizing in college classrooms. This was a carefully managed site that would post a student's account of what happened in a course only after certain standards were met: submissions had to be written and signed, and they were given to the instructor for a response before being posted together with the teacher's rebuttal. UC Berkeley's History 7B in 2003 was, a student writes, "U.S. history…as interpreted by a one-sided man who wishes to overthrow capitalism.…[He] focused excessively on negative aspects of American history to portray a country of lies and contradictions, while applauding Socialists and Anarchists.…He seemed to be more interested in creating Leftist activists than making sure students had an accurate grasp of U.S. History." The instructor "politicized every aspect of this course" and made "demonic human beings out of those who did not share his political views," in particular insisting that those who did not support affirmative action were simply racists. "His total neglect for reasonable arguments was disgusting," the student concluded.

We might wonder whether this instructor was perhaps some inexperienced young lecturer? Quite the reverse: he held a prestigious named chair, was a president of the Organization of American Historians, and won campus teaching awards. Evidently he was a leading figure in one of the nation's most prominent history departments. He was thus not atypical, but rather a celebrated member of the department, and UC Berkeley's History 7 was his longtime teaching specialty. Apparently, it is precisely by virtue of this kind of irrational, out-of-control performance that professors of history now become celebrated by their peers.

The professor offered no rebuttal to this student's account. It is difficult to see how he could object, since what the student said is entirely consistent with the course description written by the professor himself. The classroom political zealotry displayed here should shock everyone. When an angry political agenda dominates a course presentation, the intellectual level of that course will invariably be low. When a professor gives free rein to his one-sided political absolutism, students are not being asked—as they should be—to analyze and weigh different kinds of evidence in relation to the range of possible conclusions that can be drawn from them. When political outrage takes center stage, analysis and education are swept aside. People who are so controlled by anger that they can't analyze evidence should not be professors—and yet higher education is now staffed by thousands of them, and in the resulting climate the worse the offenders, the more their pseudo-professorial colleagues lionize them.

We plumb the depths of this corrupt teaching of the nation's history with our second example of a general survey. *A People's History of the United States* is a book by Howard Zinn,[1] who was a professor of political science at Boston University. It is among the most influential books ever written, having sold over two million copies, a number that is almost unheard of for academic nonfiction. It was a runner-up for the National Book Award, and received weighty endorsements from establishment historians such as the 2000 chairman of the American Historical Association, Eric Foner, and also Eric Hobsbawm, another highly ranked academic historian. The Amazon website calls Zinn's book a "classic national bestseller." All of which sounds most encouraging—until you actually read the book, at which point you may wonder what on earth the people who made those judgments were talking about.

First, let's look at Zinn's take on America's role in ridding the world of Nazism: "And yet, did the governments conducting this war— England, the United States, the Soviet Union—represent something significantly different, so that their victory would be a blow to imperialism, racism, totalitarianism, militarism, in the world?" he asks. And further, "did the behavior of the United States show that her war aims were humanitarian, or centered on power and profit?" Zinn's answer to his rhetorical questions is of course, no, we were just as bad: we waged the war not to stop tyranny, but because we too were greedy and power-hungry. Our *real* motives, which we disguised with so much pious talk about democracy, were to advance our own imperial ambitions. Yes, we destroyed German fascism, but "Were its essential elements—militarism, racism, imperialism—now gone? Or were they absorbed into the already poisoned bones of the victors?" In Zinn's telling, America went to work "without swastikas, goose-stepping, or officially declared racism, but under the cover of...'democracy' to advance our empire while controlling our own population."

According to Zinn, there was no essential difference between America and the Nazis. We were just better at PR than they were. But where, one might ask, is America's empire? As Colin Powell once famously said, all we asked for after the Second World War was enough ground to bury our dead. Then we went home, having liberated any number of countries from a brutal regime.

How about Zinn on the U.S. Constitution? It serves "the interests of a wealthy elite," who use it to maintain their own privileges, ingeniously "doing just enough for small property owners, for middle-income mechanics and farmers, to build a broad base of support." This is an exceedingly clever sort of manipulation by the wealthy, in Zinn's view, because "The slightly prosperous people who make up this base of support are buffers against the blacks, the Indians, the very poor whites. They enable the elite to keep control with a minimum of coercion, a maximum of law—all made palatable by the fanfare of patriotism and unity." That should set all those people straight who thought the U.S. Constitution was all about government of, by, and for the people.

The American Revolution? That too was all about our greed, as everything is for Zinn. The leaders in the fight for independence "found that by creating a nation, a symbol, a legal unity called the United States, they could take over land, profits, and political power from the favorites of the British Empire." Genuine historians often think about the American Revolution in relation to other major European revolutions: the French and the Russian. Those two led to anarchy, terror, conquest, and tyranny, while the American one did not. But for Zinn what counts is motivation: the American Revolution was motivated by greed, the French and Russian less so, he thought, and therefore they must be better. Back in the real world, any rational observer can see that the latter led to unspeakable cruelty on a grand scale, while the former led to an increasingly prosperous and uniquely successful society.

In discussing terrorism, Zinn naturally tells us that it's all our fault: "We are not hated because we practice democracy, value freedom, or uphold human rights. We are hated because our government denies these things in Third World countries whose resources are coveted by our multinational corporations." Zinn is sparing with facts to back up his sweeping claims. Most people have long since concluded that the misery of Third World countries results mostly from heavily corrupt governments. But Zinn's claims don't really originate in facts anyway—he cites very few. He sweeps aside all of the careful debate about the pros and cons of particular constitutional provisions, and shuts his eyes to the differences that anyone who is not blind can readily see between Nazism and Third World corrupt rulers on the one hand and Western democracies on the other. He peddles a conspiracy theory that is predictably spiteful for any and every historical event involving America.

One cannot come away from reading Zinn without reaching the conclusion that his book is a one-note outpouring of venom by a demented man who hates his country with an irrational fervor that will never yield to fact or argument of any kind. And yet: two million copies sold, endorsements by leading establishment academic historians, a "classic bestseller" and a very widely used textbook. All of this is surely enough to terrify any rational person. Has writing about and teaching American history really come down to irrational absurdity such as this?

In normal circumstances, Zinn's book would not be part of any serious, competent inquiry into American history. There is only one reason to mention Zinn, but unfortunately it is a compelling one: the sales figures and establishment praise for *A People's History of the United States* tell us how completely corrupt the teaching of American history has become. This incoherent nonsense is taken very seriously indeed by the radicals who now dominate the teaching of American history, because it serves their purposes.

Historical study must be something better than an exclusive focus on those aspects of a nation's development that are the least positive, subjected to the worst possible interpretations through wildly exaggerated attribution of the worst possible motives. This is not history; it is political propaganda, whose purpose is solely to make the case that the country is so rotten that it must be radically transformed. As such, it answers to neither fact nor logic.

• • •

The second major way in which campus radicals distort American history is in their failure to acknowledge the standards of behavior that prevailed in earlier times while they pass judgment on American society and practices. When campus radicals attack America as "racist" and "imperialist," they apply modern attitudes and beliefs to a time when different attitudes were the norm. They invoke moral standards that were developed over time by Europeans and use them to attack Europeans and Americans who lived at a time when almost nobody else on earth lived by those standards, and before they were fully formed. Bernard Lewis put the point very simply: "In having practiced sexism, racism and imperialism, the West was merely following the common practice of mankind throughout the millennia of recorded history."[2] To put the matter even more bluntly: Who was *not* racist by modern standards a few hundred years ago? The answer is clear: virtually nobody. But who was moving in the direction of overcoming racism and tribalism? The answer is again clear: Europeans of the Enlightenment era.

To understand just how foolish the radical account of American history is in this respect, we need to understand the Enlightenment's crucial role in changing the way people think about each other. Up to about 1800, the standard way of looking at the world was in tribal terms. People felt loyal to their local group, and didn't worry too much about the welfare of other groups; it was the business of those others to look out for themselves. This was a natural attitude in a time when most people didn't travel very far. Most would rarely have ventured beyond a limited area including their own village and the few nearby towns and villages that routine trading would take them to. Most people seldom if ever met foreigners, and few had occasion to mix with anyone not of their own race. It's understandable that people would have put more trust in those who were familiar to them.

A charge of "racism" made around the year 1800 would only have puzzled everyone. It would be silly to call people of that era racists simply because they were naturally wary of people who differed greatly from those they lived among, whether by skin color, language, or habits. In the absence of direct personal knowledge, people who never saw much beyond their own small geographical area were bound to resort to stereotypes, and those were more likely to embody fears and doubts than admiration and respect.

It was the European Enlightenment that began to cultivate a sense that we all share a common humanity, and this idea slowly replaced the tribalism of the past. A side effect was more sympathy for human suffering in general. The ingenious instruments of torture on display in the Tower of London shock the modern conscience, but the development of that conscience is part of the work of the European Enlightenment. If we want to make moral judgments about the behavior of people who lived hundreds of years ago, we must take into account the extent to which Enlightenment attitudes had penetrated that particular place at that time. If we don't, then instead of judging individuals or even whole societies, as some might wish to do, we'll really be judging the time in which they lived.

With this caveat firmly at the front of our minds, it's easy to see that American history as written by campus radical activists is nonsensical in this respect. They charge "racism" in historical contexts where nobody would have understood what that really meant. They speak as if Europeans were lagging behind everyone else in rising above tribalism, when the reverse is true: Europeans were leading the move to a sense of common humanity. The worldwide abolition of slavery was an achievement of Europeans, including those who had moved to North America. This is simply a fact of history, but radicals don't really care about being good historians. They just want something—anything—that they can use to make their case for the political transformation of America.

Ignoring the prevalence of tribalism in former times is just one of the fundamental flaws of radical history. Another is failing to take into account what is likely to happen when peoples at very different stages of development meet each other. Starting around 1800, the technological and scientific revolution lifted the standard of living of Europeans and Americans to a level that was not dreamed of in earlier times, and they shot ahead of other peoples in economic and political development. Those others have been catching up, though largely through the spread of Western technology, just as technological innovations have always spread from one culture to another sooner or later.

For Europeans of the time, experiencing a great leap forward technologically and economically, it was perfectly natural to think themselves more advanced than other cultures. We can be sure that

Africans or Chinese would have felt the same way if the leap forward had originated among them. But this is precisely where the European Enlightenment is so important: for just as their tribe was making huge advances that lifted them above others, their philosophers were promoting a view of the common humanity of all people, regardless of tribe. A paradox that completely escapes present-day campus radicals is that this novel idea is what made their accusations of "racism" possible.

The proof is that there were still many brutal tribal wars in the twentieth century in areas of the world where Enlightenment values had not penetrated. When Hutus massacred Tutsis in Rwanda, or whole populations of the Igbo were slaughtered in Nigeria, anyone who shouted "racism" would have looked like a fool. Obviously what they were seeing was pre-Enlightenment tribalism. And the same was true of the often brutal wars between different Native American tribes both before and after European settlers had arrived in North America.

The heart of the mistake that radical historians make lies in their failure to understand where their own values come from. The recent "Paris Statement" by a group of scholars that included the prominent British scholar Roger Scruton put the matter this way: "They are ignorant of the true sources of the humane decencies they themselves hold dear."[3] The system of values that underlies the charge of "racism" is European, and modern European at that. Radicals who level it against Americans of earlier times may think that they are invoking some natural system of judgment derived from simpler lifestyles like those of Native Americans, but nothing could be further from the truth. Those tribes could treat each other very badly indeed.

"Imperialism" is another charge leveled by radical historians against Americans of earlier periods without regard to the conditions of those times. Before Europeans founded the United Nations, every nation on earth had to beware of invasion by its neighbors whenever those neighbors were stronger. That being so, the only way to make your society safer was to make it as strong as possible. If England was not doing everything it could to make itself stronger in the sixteenth century, it would be losing ground to all those other countries who were, and so making itself more vulnerable to attack. England was in peril of invasion and subjugation over the years by French, Spanish, and Germans. Its empire was in part a rational response to a dangerous world, and one that paid off; after the Norman Conquest, the English were never again subjugated, while almost every other country in Europe was at one time or another. And as things turned out, the English political tradition that began with the Magna Carta and the Mother of Parliaments turned out to be well worth saving for the future benefit of the world. Historical context is important when people carelessly throw around words like "imperialism." The world was not always as it is today.

While ignoring context in order to make their harsh judgments of earlier Americans, radical historians often seem to assume that other peoples of the time were beyond reproach—an absurd fantasy. It is a great irony that campus radicals preach an absolute, no-excuses version of Enlightenment values, yet single out for attack the peoples who developed them, not those to whom they were completely foreign.

Why are radical historians so spiteful toward their own country? The answer is not hard to find. The radical left is determinedly socialist in outlook, and it detests free markets, which it pejoratively calls "capitalism." There is no doubt which of the world's nations most embodies the idea of free markets: the United States. Freed from the ancient constraints of European societies with their longstanding habits that made workplace change slower and harder, America had a much less restrictive free-market system. This is how the American economy soared so rapidly that it soon surpassed and finally dwarfed its European origins. The rise of America to world preeminence has in fact been a striking demonstration of the power of free markets, and that is precisely why campus radicals are so angry about their country. The astonishing success of the American economic system makes people with their political beliefs look foolish. Hell hath no fury like an ideologue scorned, and so the American history that the radicals write is at bottom an angry search for alibis for their own theories. If America's economic power and the affluence of its citizens can be made to seem the result of greed, racism, exploitation, and imperialism, they can go on believing in socialism.

But their explanations (greed, imperialism, racism, and so on) will never work, because they all rest on the assumption that wealth was just lying around waiting to be grabbed by greedy Americans and taken away from others. This of course is nonsense. Wealth has to be created—it doesn't pop up on its own. The poverty-stricken areas of the world were poor before Europeans or Americans arrived on their shores. America's wealth didn't come from theft, and it didn't exist before it was created by its free-market economic system. Even nations rich in natural resources still lived for centuries mainly in poverty because they didn't or couldn't exploit them: oil, for example, had no value for the countries that were rich in it until developments in the Western world gave it value. The same was true for many other commodities. Radical history that accuses America of becoming wealthy by stealing from other countries is fantasy. Genuine scholars face up to the lessons of history honestly and objectively, rather than seeking alibis in absurdities.

• • •

While they dispense ridiculous theories of American history, our colleges and universities require little of students, and consequently little is known by college graduates. A 2016 report for the American Council of Trustees and Alumni (ACTA) found that only 18 percent of liberal arts colleges have an American history course requirement for graduation. In many places, even students who major in history can graduate knowing little or nothing about the history of their own country. At UC Davis, a history major can avoid coursework in American history, and the same is true of the UC campuses at Santa Cruz, Irvine, and San Diego. UC Berkeley requires only one lower-division course (but that is 7A or 7B, of which enough has been said above), which means that a history major at the flagship UC campus could graduate knowing next to nothing about American history. It is astonishing that a subject so central to our lives as the development of our own nation from initial weakness to world preeminence culturally, militarily, and economically should be of so little interest to college professors.

A study done by ACTA in 2000 found that seniors at fifty-five of the most prestigious colleges and universities in the United States displayed astonishing ignorance of American history. When asked questions taken from a basic high school curriculum, "Four out of five—81%—of seniors from the top 55 colleges and universities in the United States received a grade of D or F. They could not identify Valley Forge, or words from the Gettysburg Address, or even the basic principles of the U.S. Constitution." This is an extraordinary level of ignorance on the part of students at highly selective institutions—colleges and universities that can recruit the best students and the best faculty in the nation. Presumably, the results could have been even worse at less selective institutions.[4]

The reason for this ignorance is clear enough: radical campus historians keep students ignorant of anything that might show the country in a positive light. But unfortunately, that includes almost all of the really distinctive things in our history—for example, America's decisive part in the Second World War, its role in the development of modern life, and the process that led to the writing of its extraordinary constitution.

The unpleasant truth is that a whole nation has handed over control of the college teaching of its history to people who have an almost deranged hostility to it.[5] They think it greedy, racist, undemocratic, and morally below other nations, but that hostility really derives from their frustration that the United States has been so successful by avoiding socialism. They are loath to mention the most central, undeniable fact of American history—that the country rose from insignificance to world leadership in an astonishingly short time. A balanced account of the nation's successes and failures would not serve their purposes; they must only find as much oppression as they can in order to make the case for drastic change. This mindset can't produce any useful knowledge about how our past relates to our present.

What do we most expect from historians? Surely, the first thing we expect is that they will set any particular event in its proper historical context, so that it can be interpreted in relation to the conditions prevailing in that context. But that's what radical historians never do. The only historical context they are interested in is that of their own time. They aren't really historians at all.

A grounding in the nation's history is one essential part of an education for citizenship, and another is a knowledge of its basic institutions, especially its constitution. Here too, recent college graduates evidently know very little. For many years, ACTA surveys have shown an astounding level of ignorance on the part of recent college graduates as to the most basic aspects of governance in the United States. The survey in 2016, justifiably entitled "A Crisis in Civic Education," calls this a grim reality, and concludes: "In a country that depends upon an educated populace, ignorance of our history and founding documents will be disastrous."[6]

The details of the ACTA surveys are striking. In a 2015 survey devoted specifically to knowledge of the U.S. Constitution, only 53 percent of college graduates knew the terms of office for U.S. senators and representatives; only 41 percent knew the process of ratification of an amendment to the Constitution; only 48 percent knew that an impeachment trial is before the U.S. Senate; and only 60 percent knew that war can be declared only by the Congress. If these figures were true of the general population they would be bad enough, but for college graduates they are disgraceful.

Similar results have been obtained by other surveys. A study by the Woodrow Wilson National Fellowship Foundation published on October 3, 2018 found that only one in three Americans could pass a multiple-choice test consisting of items taken from the U.S. Citizenship Test. Half didn't know which countries we fought against in the Second World War, and 57 percent didn't know how many justices are on the U.S. Supreme Court. This survey also underscored the crucial point that the main problem is with the more recently educated segment of the population: "Those 65 years and older scored the best, with 74 percent answering at least six in 10 questions correctly. For those under the age of 45, only 19 percent passed the exam, with 81 percent scoring at 59 percent or lower." The message is clear: education for citizenship used to be a great deal better than it is now. Even people whose education had happened forty years ago could still remember more than recent graduates knew.

Our form of government really works well only if most Americans understand how it works. They need to know what is distinctive about it and to understand how and why it came about. What made the founding fathers do what they did? And what makes the constitution they produced so different from others? It is a uniquely important document: America may be a young country, but its constitution has stood the test of time as no other has. It is the oldest still-functioning one in the world. It was the work of exceptionally thoughtful men who in spite of being mainly farmers were well informed about the political history of the world.

They had just thrown off the shackles of a monarchy, but their knowledge of history had taught them something very important: that when in the past a people had gotten rid of a tyrant, they were generally not very good at making sure they didn't soon get another one. In England, the execution of Charles I was followed by Oliver Cromwell—a zeal to get rid of tyranny led to something worse. Many centuries before, the Romans deposed Tarquin the Proud and then went to extraordinary lengths to prevent arbitrary rule by one man. Their government was to be headed by two consuls, each having the right to veto the other, while terms of office would be for one year only. That seemed a watertight way of warding off one-man tyranny, but eventually it backfired spectacularly because it created a power vacuum that attracted strongmen like Pompey, Julius Caesar, and the emperor Augustus.

Because the founding fathers knew their history so well, they thought long and hard about how to create a head of government strong enough to avoid the danger of a power vacuum but not so strong as to be able to develop into a tyranny. Their ingenious solution succeeded both because they learned the lessons of history and because they had a shrewd grasp of human nature. By contrast, the nearly contemporaneous revolution against an absolutist monarchy in France led to anarchy, soon followed by the rise of another dictator, Napoleon Bonaparte. The Americans may have been a long distance away from the ancient civilizations of Europe, but they knew enough and were smart enough to avoid the danger that France succumbed to. The country they built has also avoided the errors of Marxist revolutions, which have always failed because their leaders had no grasp of either history or human nature.

On one difficult constitutional issue after another, the founding fathers understood what the dangers were, and after long, well-informed debate they crafted solutions that were never less than intelligent, and often were absolutely inspired. The old problem of the tyranny of the majority was met by a limitation on the powers of government; the founders understood well that there was a difference between what the majority would like to do and what it had a right to do. Another difficult issue in representative government was the proper relationship between elected representatives and those they represented: were the representatives to exercise independent judgment once elected, or instead do only as their constituents wanted them to do? Again, the founders' solution was ingenious: members of the House of Representatives would serve two-year terms, while senators would have terms of six years. The former would need to keep making sure their constituents approved of what they were doing, while the latter would come to think of the national interest more broadly—or as Edmund Burke put it, to see themselves not as members for Bristol, but as members of Parliament.

The founders were heirs to the political tradition that began with the Magna Carta and the Mother of Parliaments, passing through episodes like the execution of Charles I, the experiment with a Lord Protector, the flawed return to monarchy, and the resultant Glorious Revolution of 1688. But they added their own independent thought to that tradition and so produced a unique form of government that really worked, and under which their country gained strength as no other had ever done in so short a time. Many scholars have judged *The Federalist*—the explanation of the principles of the U.S. Constitution composed by three of the founding fathers under the pseudonym Publius—to be among the greatest works of political theory ever written. The Constitution it elucidated demands our college students' attention by virtue of its proven workability and staying power, the enormous success of the country under its operation, and not least because it is *our* system of government.

Surely, the nation would be the better for having all of its citizens understand the story of and the rationale for the Constitution. And yet graduation requirements for a class that studies the U.S. Constitution have vanished almost everywhere on our politicized campuses. On many of them, undergraduate classes in the Constitution are not even available as electives.[7] The controlling faculty majority simply don't want knowledge of the nation's constitutional framework to be fostered, because it doesn't suit their purposes.

But what is the case they make against it? Here we must keep in the forefront of our minds the sheer depth of knowledge and profundity of thought that the founders brought to the task of writing a constitution. How do the campus left's arguments against it match up to this extraordinarily deep thought? What is their contribution to the complex constitutional debate? As we've seen previously, about all that they can contribute is the usual one-word charge: "racists!" The discrepancy between the complexity of thought of the founders and the crudeness and ignorance of their radical campus critics could not be greater. The question that should matter to all of us is how well did the founders solve the difficult constitutional problems they grappled with? And here campus radicals have virtually nothing to say.

The deeper reason for the radical left's rejection of the enormously successful U.S. Constitution, however, is that it interferes with what they want to do. The founders understood that however benign its intentions may be, unlimited government will sooner or later mean tyranny. But faculty radicals need a government big enough and powerful enough to fundamentally reshape society as they want it to be. You can't go beyond equality of opportunity to engineer equality of outcomes with limited government. Nor can you redistribute wealth from some people to others with a government that is forbidden to make unreasonable searches and seizures. Big government with unlimited powers is vital for socialist schemes. That's why campus radicals don't want students to study the Constitution, and why the rest of us have a large stake in making sure that they do.

With respect to their constitutional thought, campus radicals seem to be throwbacks to an earlier time, before we learned the lessons of the twentieth century—lessons that proved over and over again, in about twenty different countries, that governments with unlimited powers and good intentions are likely to become dictatorships that produce misery. Time after time, these systems allowed evil men to rise to the top: Lenin, Stalin, Mao, Mugabe, Ceausescu, the Kims, and so on. The founding fathers knew enough about human history and human nature to give us a constitution that protects us from such disasters, and from such men. By contrast, the present faculty of our colleges and universities seem incapable of learning from history—college faculty, of all people! In spite of all their obvious advantages, their thought is primitive and ill informed. It remains at a level that we should expect only of people who were never college-educated. Yet, once again, these are the people who now run our campuses. Perhaps it is as well that they no longer teach the Constitution: they'd make a hash of it.

• • •

One last category of education for citizenship is an acquaintance with the outstanding writings and crucial events in the history of our civilization. The number of books that have been published throughout history is in the millions, but a very small number of them endure. Most are soon forgotten, because they deserve to be, while a few command attention so powerfully that they are read over and over, from one generation to the next. Their quality of thought and writing makes some float to the top and remain relevant to modern life. As long as people think about liberty, they will be reading John Stuart Mill's *On Liberty*. As long as people think about war and peace, they will be reading the Greek historian Thucydides. And as long as people are interested in thinking about the dilemmas that they face in their lives, they will be reading Shakespeare, Dickens, Goethe, Tolstoy.

The best of our civilization's thought is available to each new generation through the works of extraordinary writers, thinkers, and observers of human life. There is no democracy of books. The best remain after millions of others are forgotten because they continue to grip the attention of readers. They are a part of education for citizenship, giving us the most memorable and profound commentary on life that has ever been committed to writing. One of the great privileges of higher education is the opportunity to study these magnificent works under the guidance of teachers who have a long history of thinking about them.

The enduring works of literature and philosophy and history are an important aspect of the development of our civilization, and of modern life itself, and so an acquaintance with a number of them is a vital part of a college education. Students learn from incisive thinkers and from superlative writers whose use of the English language is a model that should inspire them to write well themselves. Yet on the politicized campus this aspect of education for citizenship too is being abandoned. Again, just the bare facts of the situation are astonishing. All across the country, bachelor's degrees in English literature can be had without reading Shakespeare, Chaucer, or Milton. Books that have proved their extraordinary power to command attention from generation after generation of readers are being abandoned in favor of others that have never demonstrated that kind of staying power and are not likely to. Why? We must distinguish the arguments given for this folly from the real reasons for it.

The main argument for this abandonment of books that have been able to withstand the merciless test of time is that they are a white supremacist and mainly male collection, and that this racism and sexism must be remedied by giving minority and women writers their chance to be read too. But this argument is absurd on its face. Mill's essay did not survive because its author was a white male, but because it represented thinking of the very highest quality on an issue central to human life. Many other white males wrote on the same topic, but their white maleness was not enough to ensure that their writings would survive—they could not compete with Mill for the reading public's attention. Jane Austen's novels are still read not because she was a woman, but because she was both one of the greatest writers in the history of the English language and an extraordinary commentator on human life. Alexandre Dumas did not become the most read novelist in the French language because he was a black man whose mother was an African slave, but because he wrote stories that powerfully grip the imagination of people reading them long after his death. It would be insulting to Dumas and Austen to say that we should read their works because the authors were black and female, respectively. We read them because they are so compelling: they have earned their exceptional standing by decisively winning the battle for survival among so many other books. That's why they are an essential part of a fine education.

Their shallow modern replacements have not earned that standing. Heather Mac Donald comments trenchantly on the "relentless determination to reduce the stunning complexity of the past to the shallow categories of identity and class politics." The reason for this folly is that "the contemporary academic wants only to study oppression, preferably his own, defined reductively according to gonads and melanin."[8]

Choosing books to redress ethnic or sexual imbalances is a way to bring education down to mediocrity; it won't make for well-educated citizens. For that you need the best books available—books that challenge all students by their quality, rather than flattering some particular group or other by a superficial kinship. Who really cares if Shakespeare was a white male when he is the greatest writer in the English language? Who but a campus radical would want to drop him from a reading list in order to add a recent, soon-to-be-forgotten work by a minority writer who repetitively laments the alleged racism of our society?

It is wishful thinking to imagine that we can make up a list of great works by criteria other than an enduring respect for quality. If Mill wrote one of the greatest treatments of the idea of liberty, we must have it. If Shakespeare's are the plays that still dominate the theater after four centuries, we must have them. And if the novels of Alexandre Dumas still fascinate readers after so many years, we must have them too, for reasons of quality alone. Students deserve and should get the best—the greatest thought and the greatest writing, as proved by the test of time. Minority students certainly deserve the best too, and in fact a fine education will *really* lead to social change.

A knowledge of the crucial events in the development of modern civilization is the other part of a basic education for citizenship in the modern world. It too is now abandoned. The courses that once embodied this kind of education were called "Western Civilization," but that title, though accurate to a degree, was the wrong one. The central purpose of such courses was surely to trace the roots of our *modern* way of life, and that purpose gave them their central place in the curriculum. So we should think in terms of courses in the development of modern civilization, not just Western civilization.

To be sure, most of that story unfolded in the West, but not all: the Middle East and Asia also supplied important elements. From the Middle East came the enormously influential Jewish Bible. In India, the work of Panini (ca. 400 BC), the world's first grammarian, was important for the rise of the idea of the scholar and learned man. The most important center of cultural activity in classical times was around the

Mediterranean, but after the European Renaissance the center shifted to northern Europe. It was there that the scientific and technological revolution took place, and now it has spread worldwide and shapes life everywhere.

Which people were most responsible for the important innovations that went into this revolution is simply a matter of historical fact. And any historical narrative of how the transformation of life unfolded must of necessity describe who did what and when, and how important they were in the historical process. A true account cannot avoid giving a good deal of space and prominence to the part that northern Europeans played in the progress of the last two centuries. It's only campus radical activists who object to prominence earned by historical deeds, and want instead a kind of spurious democracy of historical events in which all are equally important.

The explanation for this unrealistic obsession is, once again, the radicals' war against their own society. They don't want to grant its accomplishments, and hence they don't want courses about the development of modern life in which the West has such a large part. They would rather leave students in a state of ignorance than give them anything that might increase their understanding of their civilization's history, because that understanding might increase their regard for it and thereby weaken the case for radical social change. To the extent that our society is shown to have any special place in the development of modern life, the radical political agenda is undermined. It's therefore in the interests of political radicals to have students ignorant about how modern life developed, but it's in *our* interests to keep the teaching of history out of the hands of people like that.

Courses in Western civilization were once required for all freshmen, but those requirements have now vanished almost everywhere. When I looked into the requirements for and availability of Western civilization courses in the University of California in 2012, I was shocked to find that none of the nine general campuses still had a campuswide requirement for such courses, and that not a single *history* department on any of the campuses required a survey course in Western civilization for a history major. Even more astonishing was that most of the campuses (the exceptions then being UCLA and UC Davis) did not even offer courses that surveyed the history of Western civilization. Had such courses been described as the development of modern life, as they should have been, it might not have been so easy to get rid of them. The title "Western Civilization" made it easier to attack them as ethnocentric. But the attack was no less irrational for that.

A doctrine that was invoked to help in the campaign to abolish Western civilization courses was the idea that all cultures are equal, that none may be judged better than any other, but merely different. This idea is currently popular almost everywhere—except that nobody really believes it. Given a choice, who would opt to live with starvation and chaos? Millions flee from some countries to seek a better life in others; those people can see perfectly well that all cultures are not equal. Only campus political zealots could think that they are. Northern Europe has spread its culture of technological innovation around the world, while the culture of Shaka Zulu has no influence anywhere.

The idea that all cultures are equal is in any case meaningless on its face. How could they possibly be equal when they are all different? This is where "cultural relativism" comes in—the idea that we must accept each culture on its own terms alone, rather than judge it against the standards of another culture. Yet campus radicals effectively abandon this principle themselves when they are so bitterly critical of their own culture. Plainly, they must realize that cultural relativism is a silly idea.

By teaching such nonsensical notions, the campus radical culture has destroyed education for citizenship. It has left us with graduates who are ignorant of the history of their own country and its institutions. They have not acquired an understanding of the history of their civilization, but instead are encouraged to entertain foolish ideas that poison their attitude to it.

CHAPTER 5

Graduates Who Know Little and Can't Think

T he previous chapter showed how the most important parts of education for citizenship have been destroyed by the radical politics that now dominates the campuses. Students learn only a distorted version of the history of their country and their civilization, one designed to induce in them a jaundiced view of their own society. And they learn nothing about the extraordinary constitution that determines how its government works. Let's turn now to some broader questions that concern how well the radical campus prepares students to function in society and in the workforce. Are they taught how to think productively, to reason, to write well? How does the present state of higher education affect the K–12 schools? And what is its general impact on the social and political life of the nation?

Everyone knows that complaints about the quality of higher education are now heard with great frequency. What is less well known is that a large number of careful studies have already investigated what college graduates have learned by the time they get their degrees. These studies have been done by all kinds of people and agencies with quite different attitudes and interests. They include employer organizations, think tanks, educational theorists, and academic researchers. But though the people who have performed these studies come at the question from different directions with differing social and political attitudes and with differing methodologies, there is very little difference in their conclusions. They all find that recent graduates seem to have been very poorly educated. One study after another has found that they write badly, can't reason, can't read any reasonably complex material, have alarming gaps in their knowledge of the history and institutions of the society in which they live, and are in general poorly prepared for the workplace.

The most interesting—and devastating—of these studies is that by Richard Arum and Josipa Roksa, whose book documenting their study, *Academically Adrift: Limited Learning on College Campuses*, appeared in 2011.[1] Arum and Roksa found that higher education in America today "is characterized by limited or no learning for a large proportion of students." More specifically, "An astounding proportion of students are progressing through higher education today without measurable gains in general skills as assessed by the CLA [Collegiate Learning Assessment]." The authors also find "at least some evidence that college students improved their critical thinking skills much more in the past than they do today."[2]

Looking at a sample of more than 2,300 students, Arum and Roksa observed "no statistically significant gains in critical thinking, complex reasoning, and writing skills for at least 45 percent of the students" tracked in their study. What is interesting here is that the two researchers seem somewhat puzzled by these results. Nonetheless, they see clearly enough that the blame must rest with the faculty—that students didn't just get dumber for no reason. Arum and Roksa think the problem must be that professors don't demand enough of students. In one sense they are right (though not in the way they probably intend), but they seem unwilling to ask why this change has happened. It can't be that faculty suddenly became lazy.

A variety of other studies confirm the findings of Arum and Roksa. In 2006 a study done jointly by four organizations looked at preparedness for the workforce from an employer's point of view. The title in itself suggested that something had gone badly wrong: *Are They Really Ready To Work? Employers' Perspectives on the Basic Knowledge and Applied Skills of New Entrants to the 21st Century U.S. Workforce.*[3] The study asked over four hundred employers for their views on the readiness of new entrants to the workforce, and reported "employers' growing frustrations over the lack of skills they see in new workforce entrants." Employers considered college graduates deficient in writing, written communications, and leadership skills. The authors reached a highly negative conclusion: "The future U.S. workforce is here—and it is woefully unprepared for the demands of today's (and tomorrow's) workplace."

Another study of the state of higher education that came to an equally disturbing conclusion was done by the National Center for Education Statistics.[4] Focusing on the literacy of adults at various educational levels, and comparing results in 2003 with those from 1992, it found a sharp decline in eleven years. Two tests were conducted. The first involved understanding and responding appropriately to short prose texts, while the second was about reading and extrapolating from complex books and documents. The results showed that college graduates' scores on short prose texts declined by 11 points, and on longer documents by 14 points, while the scores for graduate students declined by 13 and 17 points respectively. The virtue of this study is that it doesn't just give us a disappointing statistic and leave us to wonder how much better the scores ought to be. Instead, it gives us a specific score from just eleven years earlier as a reference point and thus shows an astonishing decline from a well-documented state of affairs.

These results were at first buried in the NCES website among all kinds of other statistics, and so it took an article by Lois Romano in the *Washington Post* to get the appalling conclusions noticed. Romano was in no doubt as to how much all of this should worry us:

> Literacy experts and educators say they are stunned by the results of a recent adult literacy assessment, which shows that the reading proficiency of college graduates has declined in the past decade, with no obvious explanation.... While more Americans are graduating from college, and more than ever are applying for admission, far fewer are leaving higher education with the skills needed to comprehend routine data, such as reading a table about the relationship between blood pressure and physical activity, according to the federal study conducted by the National Center for Education Statistics.[5]

One has to wonder whether anyone would have noticed this horrendous decline if Romano hadn't written her article. Her piece was reprinted and commented on many times, while almost nobody used the NCES study itself as a primary source. Romano provided more details of the test scores, but it was left to a man that she interviewed to put his finger on the real horror of what the NCES had uncovered:

> Only 41 percent of graduate students tested in 2003 could be classified as "proficient" in prose—reading and understanding information in short texts—down 10 percentage points since 1992. Of college graduates, only 31 percent were classified as proficient—compared with 40 percent in 1992. "It's appalling—it's really astounding," said Michael Gorman, president of the American Library Association and a librarian at California State University at Fresno. "Only 31 percent of college graduates can read a complex book and extrapolate from it. That's not saying much for the remainder."

Gorman is correct: it is indeed astounding that 69 percent of college graduates apparently can't read any reasonably complex material with an acceptable level of understanding, and even more astonishing that 41 percent of candidates for *higher degrees* are not proficient in reading!

But what of Romano's claim that there is no obvious explanation for this collapse of test scores for college graduates? There is a perfectly obvious explanation. The period from 1992 to 2003 was the crucial time when the politicization of the nation's college and university faculties suddenly gained enormous momentum, the result being that an already pronounced tilt to the left quickly turned into the virtually one-party campus. Can it really be a coincidence that the literacy of college graduates plunged disastrously at the same time?

If graduates show serious ignorance of the history and political institutions of the society in which they live, that is exactly what one should have expected when campus requirements in American history and institutions and in Western civilization were abolished, and when there is so much faculty hostility to such courses. If graduates can't even write short declarative sentences competently, that is not surprising when writing courses neglect the skill of writing and focus instead on radical politics, as they now often do. When graduates can't read and extrapolate from books of any reasonable level of difficulty, that is just what one would expect when reading lists so often give them books written at the superficial level of journalism rather than more complex works that would really challenge them, as used to be the case. This is what happens when great books that have stood the test of time are abandoned in favor of politically correct simplemindedness.

If students have not learned to reason and to analyze, what else should we expect when they are so often asked simply to adopt a radical political viewpoint, instead of analyzing complex issues for themselves? If students were asked to evaluate different political stances they would have to think about them, but when they are pressured to accept one position they are in effect being told to *stop* thinking. A common defense of this practice by radical activists is that students are being challenged when confronted by a system of political beliefs very different from that which they bring to the classroom. But students won't learn how to think and analyze if they are simply pressed to substitute one dogmatic belief system for another. What a college-level education must provide is the analytical skill to dissect and evaluate ideas—*any* ideas. But that kind of education would not serve the interests of political radicals. They want followers and supporters, not people who give serious thought to whatever cause they are pressured to join. If students think for themselves, they might make a decision that is not what the radicals want.

It's surely obvious that there is a close connection between the shortcomings of recent graduates, shown by many studies, and the politicization of the campuses. The former are the predictable consequences of the latter. When academia fails to provide a large proportion of its students with either analytical skills or useful knowledge, that represents enormous losses for the nation. Aside from the waste of four years and of a great deal of money there is the missed opportunity both for students and for the rest of us. They don't get a college education, and we don't get an informed citizenry. The damage is not just to those who don't learn anything at all. The better students show some improvement in their writing and reasoning skills, but they still receive the same inferior teaching that produced no gains at all for so many.

The studies we've looked at so far give most of their attention to the large numbers of college graduates who have learned little or nothing while at college. But what do we know about the more accomplished students—what have they learned? Not nearly enough, according to a member of the committee to select Rhodes Scholars, that is, the best of the college graduates. In an article in the *Washington Post* for January 23, 2011 ("Our Superficial Scholars"), Heather Wilson, who has the broad perspective acquired by twenty years of service on that committee, reported that even high-achieving students now "seem less able to grapple with issues that require them to think across disciplines or reflect on difficult questions about what matters and why." She and the committee look for "students who wonder, students who are reading widely," but "the undergraduate education they are receiving seems less and less suited to that purpose." Wilson gave four examples of what she meant by this:

> An outstanding biochemistry major wants to be a doctor and supports the president's health-care bill but doesn't really know why. A student who started a chapter of Global Zero at his university hasn't really thought about whether a world in which great powers have divested themselves of nuclear weapons would be more stable or less so, or whether nuclear deterrence can ever be moral. A young service academy cadet who is likely to be serving in a war zone within the year believes there are things worth dying for but doesn't seem to have thought much about what is worth killing for. A student who wants to study comparative government doesn't seem to know much about the important features and limitations of America's Constitution.

These recent graduates were among the very best of their time, but they seemed to Wilson noticeably less accomplished than those seen by the committee in past years.

We've seen abundant evidence that the one-party politicized

campus does not and cannot teach students to reason, to write, or to read anything complex with adequate understanding, and that it produces graduates with dismaying gaps in their general knowledge and particularly in knowledge of their own society's governance and history. All of which is certainly alarming. But the level of our alarm should rise even higher when we contemplate one simple fact: teachers in high schools and elementary schools are all trained in colleges and universities. This should suggest that we are likely to find a corresponding deterioration in teaching at those levels too. And we do. The rot of higher education has spread to the K–12 schools and now undermines our whole educational system.

Complaints about the quality of education in the high schools are now so common that they are no longer news. Even the college faculty who have so poorly educated the nation's schoolteachers complain bitterly about incoming freshmen being inadequately prepared for college. Arum and Roksa found that "40 percent of college faculty agree with the statement: 'Most of the students I teach lack the basic skills for college level work.'"[6] It seems never to occur to the complaining college faculty that this must ultimately be their own fault—for where else do high school teachers get their education? While there is broad agreement that teaching in K–12 schools has deteriorated greatly in recent years, the question of who trained the teachers is always missing from the complaints.

An independent nonprofit education reform organization that the nation's governors and corporate leaders set up, called Achieve, published a report in 2005 saying that college instructors "are the harshest critics of public high schools." Nearly half (48 percent) are dissatisfied with the preparation that students are receiving in American public high schools, according to the report. More specifically,

> Large majorities of instructors are dissatisfied with the job public high schools are doing in preparing students for college when it comes to writing quality (62%) and their ability to read and comprehend complex materials (70%). Majorities of instructors are dissatisfied with their preparation in a number of other areas, including their ability to think analytically (66%), their work and

study habits (65%), their ability to do research (59%), applying what they learn to solve problems (55%) and mathematics (52%).[7]

Today, an astounding proportion of the students entering higher education must take remedial courses when they begin, which means that they are not prepared for college-level work even in terms of minimal formal requirements. In the California State University system, for example, over half of all entrants must do remedial work. In other words, less than half of those entering the system are even minimally prepared for college. Why are teachers in high schools and elementary schools not doing a better job of preparing their students for higher education?

A major part of the problem lies in the schools of education that credential teachers, as Rita Kramer found when she undertook the research documented in her devastating book *Ed School Follies: The Miseducation of America's Teachers*, published in 1991.[8] Kramer's research showed convincingly that the low quality of the public schools was the result of the political preoccupations that animated teacher training in the nation's colleges. She visited numerous schools of education across the country, studying and evaluating how they prepared their students for teaching careers. She found an astonishing uniformity of opinion on one central issue:

> The goal of schooling is not considered to be instructional, let alone intellectual, but political.... The public school, once charged with the task of transmitting the common culture and imparting the skills required to understand it, participate in it, and extend it, has come to be seen instead by those who prepare men and women to teach in it as an agency of social change.

Kramer also found that the low level of skills and knowledge in the public schools was strongly correlated with the politicization of university ed-school programs. Worse still, she discovered that the well-documented ignorance of the nation's history and its institutions among high school graduates was the intended result of a conscious policy choice rather than of neglect. Schools of education "denigrate the history of the institutions that made us the nation that we are," Kramer found. Further, "Any knowledge or appreciation of that common culture and the institutions from which it derives, I found conspicuously absent in the places that prepare men and women to teach in our country's public schools today." Her final judgment was that we need to "place knowledge itself at the center of the educational enterprise" if we are going to have better teachers and better schools.

Kramer's recognition that a clear policy choice lies at the root of the problem is highly important, because when anyone notices that our schoolchildren are doing badly, it is often assumed that this must be happening because teachers are ineffective or neglectful. For example, a study of education done in California in 2011 found the same distressing results we've already seen in other studies, but its title immediately spelled out an interpretation for which there was no basis in fact: "Consequences of Neglect: Performance Trends in California Higher Education."[9] Yet it wasn't neglect that made California at that time thirty-ninth among all the states in its share of eighth graders who scored at the proficient level or better on the National Assessment of Educational Progress. This result might seem strange when set against the fact that California has the most developed and prestigious system of state-funded universities and colleges in the world. But this is what happens when that powerful system of higher education is spreading dysfunction and political radicalism instead of knowledge and mental acuity. When college campuses stop teaching students how to think and instead tell them what ideology they must commit to, that dereliction of duty trickles down to the high schools and produces the same kinds of disaster in both places.

Rita Kramer's study of education schools is now nearly thirty years old, but more recent work confirms that nothing has improved in the meantime. Jay Schalin looked at three major university education schools and compiled a list of the ten authors whose works were the most frequently assigned in courses. He found that every person on that list "is highly political and holds beliefs far to the left of ordinary liberals." More generally, Schalin concluded: "Teacher education has become one of the most politicized corners of academia, an institution that is already out of step with the rest of the country politically."[10]

To summarize: students who graduate from the heavily politicized radical campus cause yet more educational destruction by importing the same incompetent and politicized teaching into the public schools.

• • •

Severe damage to our entire educational system is only part of the harm that the one-party campus does. It damages our society in many other ways, not the least of which is sabotaging the path to advancement for underprivileged and minority students.

Access to first-rate higher education—genuine, uncorrupted higher education—has always been a powerful force for social justice in the broadest sense. Education is the great leveler. Nothing has done more for opportunity in our society than an excellent system of higher education. Historically, it has propelled whole groups of have-nots to full equality. Not so very long ago, large populations of recent immigrants—Italians, Irish, Jews—began life in America as the downtrodden poor, but access to first-rate public education enabled them to become fully integrated into American society and to enjoy all of its blessings. Excellent public education was the engine of social change for these large immigrant populations in earlier generations, and soon enough the result was senators, Supreme Court justices, and even U.S. presidents from those populations.

The point can't be stressed enough: excellence in higher education has been a highly effective engine of social change for large groups of people who were once the country's have-nots but are now well represented at every social stratum and in every walk of American life. It really produced results. But it worked only because it was real education, not the sham offered by the present diversity regime on campus. Students were given a thorough grounding in the accumulated knowledge and wisdom of their civilization. They became genuinely educated people who as a consequence were able to move upward. A diploma was important only because it represented the level of education that an individual had reached; the skills and knowledge that the diploma represented were what really made opportunity possible.

A measure of optimism was crucial to this process: a belief in the essential fairness and effectiveness of the system overall, despite some obvious pockets of unfairness. Students had to believe that it was worthwhile for them to work hard to master ideas and knowledge, because their mastery would be recognized and would equip them for rewarding careers.

At any particular historical moment, the people who have the greatest stake in excellence in public higher education are those looking to move up the social scale—the have-nots of their time. This means that if public higher education is now seriously deficient in any respect, the groups most harmed will be ethnic minorities, because those are the people who need it most at this particular moment. In recent decades our society has recognized the need to empower black students to climb the social ladder by means of higher education, as Italians, Irish, and Jews had done before them. But just when they needed it to lift them to full equality, it was no longer there for them. And it was the campus political radicals who took it from them, even as those radicals claimed to be their friends and supporters.

These last decades have made it abundantly clear that higher education cannot have direct social and political goals without becoming seriously corrupted. Paradoxically, something that the politicized campus prides itself on—the advancement to full equality of minorities—has been severely impeded as a result. The domination of higher education by radical political activists has been a tragedy for black students, and this is a national scandal.

The crux of the matter is that control of the education that should have led to full equality in the mainstream of our society is now in the hands of people who loathe that mainstream. The kind of education that in past generations has elevated low-status immigrant groups would stand in the way of the radicals' social agenda by strengthening the status quo, which they want instead to weaken. To move up, minority students need to attain mastery of their civilization's accumulated knowledge, but political radicals don't look at the history of their society and see knowledge and wisdom; they see only a record of oppression. They have no great respect for its institutions or achievements, and they want to make sure that their students don't either. Those radicals are alienated from their own society and they want to infect their students with that alienation—even when in the case of black students that will take away their precious chance of climbing the ladder. We should be under no illusion: campus political radicals are a thoroughly selfish group who never stop to think who is being damaged by their pursuit of power.

Radical activists sabotage and derail minority student progress in numerous ways. By telling minorities that racism is still undiminished everywhere, they undermine confidence that trying to succeed is worthwhile. By denigrating society as it is, they undermine a desire to seek a better place in it. By dismantling the coursework that would give minority students mastery of their society's history and institutions, they prevent their acquisition of that mastery. By telling minority students that they should be reading writers ethnically similar to themselves, they cut them off from the wisdom of the great writers of the past and steer them instead toward minor figures who like themselves are alienated and obsessed with racism. When minority students are told that it is to their advantage to read mediocre writers who have not stood the test of time instead of writers of the stature of Shakespeare, they are betrayed. All of this destroys black educational opportunity and is a recipe not for minority success, but for failure.

For minorities, the transformation of the curriculum by radical activists has been nothing short of catastrophic. When Jesse Jackson marched with students at Stanford University chanting "Hey Hey, Ho Ho, Western Civ has got to go,"[†] he was helping to destroy the chance of upward mobility for the groups that he claimed to be leading and championing. He was putting a rigorous, well-rounded education in the great classic writers and thinkers out of their reach just when they needed it most. And the resulting dumbing down of the education of high school teachers guaranteed that black students would arrive at college with a handicap every bit as great as it has ever been. Denying black students a mastery of the way that modernity came about was denying them a fair chance of advancement. When you see high black unemployment, especially young black male unemployment, blame campus radicals. An old test of any action is: *cui bono?* In whose interests

---

† In some accounts the wording of this chant was slightly different: "Western Culture's got to go." The wording in the text seems the most likely.

is it? Alienation from their society, ignorance of its development, its achievements, and its essential nature may be in the interests of radical zealots, but it is absolutely not in the interests of black students. College administrators who talk endlessly about diversity imagine that they are nobly supporting minority students when they are actually selling them out. Black students on the way to getting an excellent college education are in effect being waylaid by political radicals intent on diverting them from that goal to use them for their own purposes.

Not only are black students not moving up—they are actually losing ground as the gap between them and other students is increasing. This is another of the dreadful findings of the research by Arum and Roksa. It was already well known that African American students enter higher education with much lower Collegiate Learning Assessment (CLA) scores than do their white counterparts. But Arum and Roksa found that "During their first two years of college, white students gained 41 CLA points, while African-American students gained only 7 points.... As a consequence, the gap between African-American and white students increased over time."

It's worth dwelling on this sad result. Higher education should be closing the gap between black and white students. Instead, it's increasing the gap: black students slip further behind their white counterparts because of their college experience. That development is so devastating for the future of our society that it ought to make everyone drop what they are doing right now and devote themselves to reversing it, but that won't happen; and it won't happen because the people who are doing it don't really care about anything but their own selfish political goals.

As we saw in an earlier chapter, racial preferences in student admissions damage minority students through the "mismatch" effect, but the full extent of the damage goes well beyond that. Preferences are often said to be needed only because minority students so often get a defective high school education. If that is indeed the case, it's because their high school teachers themselves are no longer well educated. And the main reason they are not is that campuses have elevated "diversity" over excellence, in faculty hiring and student admissions and in curriculum. The diversity agenda increases political radicalism, which is the very force that undermines college education and thus leads to even more poorly prepared high school teachers. We have here a classic vicious circle: the minority high school deficit leads to preferences in college admissions, preferences lead to political radicalism on campus, campus radicalism leads to a deterioration in the education of high school teachers, more poorly educated high school teachers increase the minority deficit, and that leads to even greater demands for preferences. Though the intent of college admissions preferences is to provide upward mobility for minorities, what they really do is reduce the quality of a college education by promoting a force that cripples it.

Another way in which the prospects for the advancement of black students are damaged by the radicalized campus lies in the creation of departments that from their inception have been hotbeds of alienated radicalism, namely, departments such as Black Studies. These departments were often instituted as a response to demands from a few black students, ostensibly as a recognition of and gift to them. Nothing could be more self-defeating than these "gifts." Those departments simply keep black students out of major fields with real content and mire them even deeper in the alienated radicalism that impedes their progress. There they will be at the mercy of racial ideologues who whip up more alienation with endless racial harangues that teach them nothing of value while preventing them from learning anything else. What our society needs is black mathematicians, lawyers, chemists, and simply citizens well educated in the knowledge and traditions of the civilization of which they are a part. Black Studies programs generate only grievance and alienation that interfere with those goals. Far from promoting what we as a society need, they sabotage it. Nothing has damaged black progress toward full equality as much as control of the campuses by political radicals who have preyed upon them and used them as cannon fodder in their war against their own society.

• • •

It is sometimes said that the ranting of politically radical faculty on college campuses does little harm because students see through it and laugh at the folly. And that may well be true for many students, though it should not reassure us to think that they are having so much of their time at college wasted by fools. However, it is far from true that all students see through it. Unscrupulous proselytizing radicals have enough influence on the more easily led students to change the political complexion of the nation to a significant degree, and this is by no means the least of the harms that the politicized campuses have done to our nation.

A Gallup poll published on August 13, 2018 found that in the Democratic Party a comfortable majority (57 percent) now have a positive view of socialism, and that they outnumber those with a positive view of capitalism by a full 10 percentage points. According to Gallup's press release, this was the "first time in Gallup's measurement over the past decade that Democrats viewed socialism more favorably than capitalism." Even worse is that on this question the percentage for the 18–29 group overall (not restricted by party) is now 51 percent. We must always remember that this climate of opinion is still building: as years go by, a larger and larger percentage of the population will have had a radicalized college education. And there can be no doubt that when campus radicals talk about socialism, what they mean is generally not the political system of Norway, for example, which is a free-market (thus capitalist) country with a well-developed social welfare system, but rather the kind of socialism rooted in the ideas of Karl Marx.

These figures should really make us sit up and take notice: more than half of 18-to-29-year-olds now look favorably on a political system that has brought misery wherever it has been tried, while their own country has achieved remarkable success by avoiding that mistake. It is a system so unpopular with people who live under it that brutal dictatorships rely on violence to keep it in place when their own people come to understand what it really amounts to.

There is nothing wrong with teaching about socialism; indeed it should be taught. It has been a major factor in the history of the last century and so it should be thoroughly understood by college graduates. Teaching it should mean, here as anywhere, a hard look at the arguments for and against, an examination of both its core tenets and its variant versions, a comparison of this political theory with its competitors, and above all a careful scrutiny of the historical record of how it has fared whenever it has been implemented. And that record, as any reasonably well-informed person should know, has been so disastrous that it has been discarded by almost all nations that have tried it.

When we now see a sudden surge in enthusiasm for this almost completely discredited system of government, it must be obvious that socialism is not really being taught—not being analyzed to promote greater understanding of it, but rather *preached* on the campuses. Students are kept innocent of the disastrous history of socialism, and brainwashed into believing that it will give them a wonderful life, which it never has. Education informs, but indoctrination must keep students ignorant.

Some observers play down the importance of all this when they tell us that we shouldn't be too frightened by the large numbers of young people who are now enthusiastic about socialism, because they don't really understand what they are saying. Yes, indeed, they don't. They can't, because if they did understand, it's unlikely that they would have these beliefs. But should it really be of any comfort to us that a majority of our young people are so abysmally ignorant of matters regarding which they have such resolute beliefs? Surely not. The fact that so many have absorbed this destructive ideology on campus without understanding what it really means matters a great deal, and is a scandal of immense proportions.

It can scarcely be doubted that indoctrination by unscrupulous radicals is now having a major effect on national politics. It has changed the entire shape of the Democratic Party, which as a consequence has taken a sharp turn to the left. And the character of that change is exactly what the SDS manifesto envisaged so long ago. Such a radical change in the national political scene could not have been accomplished by a bad actor here and there in the classroom. It could only have happened through the widespread, systematic abuse of campus classrooms for political advantage on the part of very large numbers of proselytizing radical leftists.

Only a few years ago, Senator Bernie Sanders was a man that no one took very seriously as a viable figure on the national scene: he was openly socialist at a time when to most people that seemed to be the outlook of a dunce. But to everyone's surprise he very nearly took the Democratic Party nomination for president in 2016. How could this have happened? Sanders got very large numbers of votes from the campuses and from recent graduates. Since then a young woman (Alexandria Ocasio-Cortez) who displays deep ignorance on almost any topic she speaks about took the party's nomination for a congressional seat from a senior Democratic congressman *because* she pronounced herself a radical socialist. While she won a democratic election, its outcome no doubt owed much to the leftist control of college classrooms—a means by which radicals are achieving what they could not have done by democratic means alone.

The effect of campus radicalism on national politics is not limited to this leftward shift of the Democratic Party. The entire political climate of the country has become significantly harsher and more divisive. To understand how this has happened we need only look at how the political monopoly on campus is sustained. Politics usually means debate, and where there are two opposing sets of arguments, both proceeding by reason and appeals to evidence, the outcome can never be predicted. From the radicals' point of view that is a bad situation, and so they routinely seek to scuttle debate by painting one side of the argument as evil and ethically subhuman. If they succeed in doing that, they can prevent the other side of the argument from seeing the light of day on campus, and the political monoculture will be maintained. Right-of-center voices are a danger to a radical politics that is logically fragile, so those voices must be vilified before they can have any effect. The political life of the campus must be poisoned in order to sustain the one-party monopoly. And it is precisely this kind of poison that is spreading into the political life of the nation, which is why our national political culture is now more spiteful and hostile than it has been for some time. There too, right-of-center voices are often treated as if criminal.

The impact of this increasingly nasty political culture is felt in many areas of our lives. A study of the tech industry recently found that it was so dominated by hostile and intolerant left-wing employees that (according to the executive summary of the study) most center-right tech professionals "cannot bring their whole selves to work." They "feel their views are at odds with the cultural norms in their workplaces," and "cannot do their best work because their ideological views are at odds with their workplace norms."[11] This is extraordinary, and new. To be sure, individuals with differing political views have always argued about them, but an organized workplace culture of bitter ideological hatred toward the politics of half the country is unheard of. "What do you call a Silicon Valley Republican who wants to have friends?" asked Eliot Kaufman. The answer: "A Libertarian."[12] Who can doubt that the ultimate source of this animosity toward anything right of center is the political hatreds cultivated on the one-party radical-left campus?

Even a field such as medical training is feeling the impact of this intolerance: in the *Weekly Standard*, Devorah Goldman reported on campus-style obligatory leftism in the Association of American Medical Colleges:

> One MCAT [Medical College Admissions Test] practice question (from a collaboration between the AAMC and online-education nonprofit Khan Academy), for example, asks whether the wage gap between men and women is the result of bigotry, sexism, racism, or biological differences; no other options are provided, and the "correct" answer is sexism. Another asks whether the "lack of minorities such as African Americans or Latinos/Latinas among university faculty members" is due to symbolic racism, institutional racism, hidden racism, or personal bias. The "correct" answer is institutional racism. Yet another asks test-takers to select from a list of debatable definitions for the terms "sex" and "gender."[13]

It is astonishing to see such heavily partisan and logically dubious articles of faith given the status of unquestionable truth. The AAMC must know that what it offers as "correct" answers are at best highly controversial. This attempted brainwashing and bullying of a captive audience is surely straight from the one-party campus.

Further evidence of politicized medical education in America appeared in a *Wall Street Journal* article by Stanley Goldfarb, a former associate dean of the University of Pennsylvania medical school. Goldfarb drew attention to the American College of Physicians' forays into the politics of social justice and reported that medical students are increasingly having time that should be devoted to their medical education taken up with coursework on "climate change, social inequities, gun violence, bias and other progressive causes only tangentially related to treating illness."[14] But what the *Journal*'s readers must have found even more chilling than the article itself was the rebuttal letter written by Robert McLean, president of the American College of Physicians. Readers may have expected that a rebuttal would try to show that Goldfarb was exaggerating if not outright fabricating what was happening in medical schools. Not a bit of it: McLean wrote to boast that he was proud of what Goldfarb described, thus confirming that it was all true. Will we next see the appointment of an associate dean for social justice in a medical school? But it's not wise to joke about this, because that's exactly what the Keck School of Medicine at the University of Southern California has done.

The radicalized campus is spreading its tentacles into more and more areas of national life. Radical leftism dominates in state bar associations and even in many philanthropic foundations. Journalism schools have made that profession more brazenly partisan than it has ever been. Even art schools are now politicized, as Michael J. Pearce has described: "In art schools dominated by politically motivated professors, social justice activism dominates the work of many students, who can feel pressured into acting and working just like their mentors." One result is an increase in dropout rates and in school closures. Pearce asks pointedly, "Why would a student interested in an art career want to pay for a degree that leads to a job in political campaigning or unemployment?"[15]

The politicizing of academia has a multitude of far-reaching consequences. The distinguished economist Walter Williams sums up the effect on our culture trenchantly, but not unfairly:

> Many of the nation's colleges have become a force for evil and a focal point for the destruction of traditional American values. The threat to our future lies in the fact that today's college students are tomorrow's teachers, professors, judges, attorneys, legislators, and policymakers. A recent Brookings Institution poll suggests that nearly half of college students believe hate speech is not protected by the First Amendment. Of course, it is. Fifty-one percent of students think that it's acceptable to shout down a speaker with

whom they disagree. About 20 percent of students hold that it's acceptable to use violence to prevent a speaker from speaking. Over 50 percent say colleges should prohibit speech and viewpoints that might offend certain people. Contempt for the First Amendment and other constitutional guarantees is probably shared by the students' high school teachers, as well as many college professors. Brainwashing and indoctrination of young people has produced some predictable results, as shown by a recent Gallup poll. For the past 18 years, Gallup has asked adults how proud they are to be Americans. This year, only 47 percent say they are "extremely proud," well below the peak of 70 percent in 2003. The least proud to be Americans are nonwhites, young adults, and college graduates.[16]

If Williams is correct, the nation must find a way to repair this heavily corrupted higher education. With every day, the damage done to the country by the politicized one-party campus increases. The problem is not simply that we are spending a fortune on higher education with little to show for it in the way of educational benefits. Overshadowing even the enormously serious question of the time and money being wasted is the damage to the social fabric of the nation and to its political life. Before we consider some possible remedies, we'll look deeper into the condition of the campuses to see what miserable places they have really become.

CHAPTER 6

The Wretched State of the Campuses

I began my career as a university teacher over fifty years ago. I remember well how cheerful it was at the beginning of each academic year to see eager young faces about to begin their university education, and to think that they would always look back fondly on this time as one that stretched their mental capacities and made them more thoughtful and knowledgeable people. It seemed to me a great privilege to be a part of that. More generally, I felt privileged to live among sharp and thoughtful colleagues who were explorers in their fields. They were open-minded because they could not be otherwise if they were to bring new light to old problems, an essential part of their job. It was their responsibility to get their students to think in that way too. A university was then an enterprise that was easy to believe in, and to be proud of.

Few people now have that same feeling. Where faculty were formerly open-minded explorers, they are now too often closed-minded zealots. Where once the general impression of life on campus was of thoughtfulness, intelligence, and an eagerness to learn, what stands out now are episodes of extraordinary foolishness.

In the past, virtually everyone agreed that universities needed to be protected from political influence because it would corrupt them. That consensus is now gone. Today's campuses are so predominantly and brazenly left-activist that nobody could regard them as politically neutral. The entire campus atmosphere is openly political, and radical proselytizing is central to campus life. Certain ideas may be expressed freely; others may not, because they offend campus orthodoxy. As a consequence, the entire campus atmosphere is inhibited, uncertain, even fearful.

James Freeman reports the results of a study finding that a majority of students said that their professors or instructors "have used class time to express their own social or political beliefs that are completely unrelated to the subject of the course."[1] Professors are evidently making their political views part of the classroom climate, and a majority of students said they felt intimidated about expressing views different from those of their professors. Thinking for oneself in these classrooms is clearly felt to be dangerous. College classrooms, of all places.

But it's not only instructors that students fear to offend; they even self-censor to avoid offending other students too. Frank Furedi reports on a survey published by the *Harvard Crimson* which found that "around two-thirds of students who were surveyed had 'at some point chosen not to express an opinion in an academic setting out of fear that it would offend others.' The survey indicated that 78 percent of registered Republicans said they 'withheld opinions in class' compared to 59 percent of registered Democrats and 73 percent of registered Independents."[2] This self-silencing goes well beyond the normal shyness of many students—it reflects a climate of fear in which students keep quiet about their beliefs for fear of retaliation. And that does real damage to an education, for as Furedi observes, "it is through articulating an opinion and being prepared to engage in a discussion around it that students develop their ideas and acquire a measure of intellectual independence."

Politically, the campuses are quite unlike the wider world that surrounds them: they form artificial oases of political conformity and intolerance. And this makes them thoroughly wretched places to be for anyone who still cares about the academic values of disinterested inquiry, open debate, and disciplined thinking. Numerous topics are simply avoided for fear of attracting a vicious hate campaign; there are hordes of political zealots masquerading as professors; and there are legions of cowardly administrators so fearful of confronting the wrongdoers that they let them do as they wish. Students often report that particular courses require them to sit through their instructors' endless political rants and learn to regurgitate harebrained political beliefs in order to pass a course, something that should make any genuine academic despair. Defenders of the status quo often protest that there is still much on campus that is not like this, seemingly not realizing that in so doing they have just admitted that there is indeed a great deal that is.

The prevalence of a militant radical politics on campus does much more than produce an ugly atmosphere that stifles learning. It has fundamentally changed how the university works and how it relates to the broader society which it supposedly serves and of which it is a part. As a result, academia no longer fulfills many of the functions that were always expected of it.

• • •

Let's first of all look at one important respect in which there has been a complete reversal in the way that academia and society interact. Universities used to be places where the major political and social issues of the day could be researched, debated, and analyzed. The results of this careful thought and analysis could then be used to make political debates that were taking place in the wider world more realistic, more factual, and better informed. The universities of the past would have contributed importantly to national debates over issues that are contentious today, such as the real-world consequences of raising the minimum wage, the practical results of racial preferences in college admissions and faculty hiring, the possible reasons for low numbers of women in high-tech fields, and so on. The combative and partisan political style of off-campus debate would have been moderated and improved by the more careful and fact-based research of academic scholars.

Consider the example of increasing the minimum wage: politicians to the left are naturally attracted to the idea because it directs more money to the poor, while politicians to the right are wary of the risks of increased unemployment, which might actually result in making the poor still poorer. But the question whether the poor are actually hurt or helped is a factual one, and well-designed research could tell us what actually happens. Nonpartisan academic work on the subject could help people in the wider world make better decisions. This was certainly one of the ways in which universities justified their existence.

Sadly, this aspect of the relationship between academia and society is now the reverse of what it used to be. If, for example, you are interested in knowing whether racial preferences actually help or harm those they are intended to benefit, you should probably not try to pursue it on campus. Where this issue is concerned, it is the campus that is governed by emotion, partisan anger, and intolerance. Off campus, you can still discuss in a rational way what the *real* effects of racial preferences in college admissions are, and how different those real effects are from the intended results; but on campus you will be shouted down and threatened if you even raise the question. In fact, to say that the relation of the campus to the broader society is now reversed actually understates the problem. The wider world used to listen to and appreciate careful empirical research from the campus, but the present-day campus will angrily reject empirical research that violates its rigid political beliefs *wherever* that research comes from.

The campus used to pride itself on being better than the undisciplined political street, with its unreflective slogans, caricatures, and personal attacks. But it now goes much further in that direction than the partisan politics of the wider world ever did, with character assassination, hysterical accusations of racism, shouting down and silencing, and even career termination for those who challenge campus orthodoxy. That is the measure of how completely the academy has abandoned its former role in relation to the wider world.

This reversal can be seen everywhere. Take the question whether police make a habit of targeting black males, even to the extent of unjustified killings. The academic way of dealing with such a matter would formerly have been to reach immediately for relevant statistics. How many black men are killed by police? How many white men are killed by police? What are the crime rates for each group? Does the rate at which arrests result in conviction differ between white and black males? And much more of the kind. When the academic researchers of former times had assembled all the relevant statistics, they would have been in a position to say whether or not it was really true that police target black males and kill them unjustifiably. This hitherto standard academic way of deciding matters would rarely have been controversial, because if one academic mismanaged or misinterpreted the statistics, another would soon be there to correct him.

So why doesn't someone on campus do the analysis? To answer that, we need only look at what happened when Heather Mac Donald brought to the campus the results of the statistical work that should have been done on the campus. As we've seen, she was shouted down on two different campuses. Far from wanting to find the truth of whether police target black men, radical pseudo-academics actually prevented Mac Donald from bringing the analysis to the campus. Their mantra "black lives matter" was the end of the matter for them. Only one answer was to be permitted on campus: cops are racists, whatever the facts say. That unshakable belief means that anyone who wants to analyze the factual record of what has really been happening must be dismissed as a racist, and silenced. Academic analysis is now not to be permitted in academia itself! Why should citizens and taxpayers maintain these highly expensive institutions if they are now not allowed to do what they are supposed to be there for?

There is perhaps no single issue that more clearly illustrates the reversal of academia's relation to society than that of possible differences of temperament and/or aptitude between men and women. Off campus it's a question that fascinates people everywhere. On campus, nobody is even permitted to mention the subject. As we have seen, merely a cautious acknowledgment that nobody really knows what the truth is got Larry Summers fired from his Harvard presidency. On this point the campus has its orthodoxy, and it's brutally vindictive to anyone who gets out of line.

From a logical standpoint, the campus truth is very strange. If I wanted to prove whether or not women and men react to the same kind of situation in ways that are characteristically and measurably different, I'd have to design an experiment with great care. Managing all of the many variables in any human situation so that the design of an experiment focuses uniquely on only one of those variables is extremely difficult. Reaching a firm conclusion would take careful planning and hard thought. And all of that would only have illustrated one particular area of potentially different responses on the part of males and females.

Many more such experiments would be needed to test a range of possible male/female differences, until at last a more general conclusion could be abstracted from them.

What makes the campus feminist orthodoxy so strange is that it assumes the answer to this question to be very, very easy to reach: feminist radicals feel that they can say immediately and with great certainty that there are simply no differences of temperament or aptitude between men and women. And that conclusion is presented to us without mention of any empirical research: we are simply to accept that there are no differences whatever, and that is that. But wait: where actually is the work and the reasoning that determined this? It's a very strong conclusion, and making such a claim with absolute certainty ought to presuppose very extensive research. *But there is no such research.* So here we have a very sweeping claim advanced as an absolute certainty, one so complete, so definite, so exclusive that no questioning of it is possible or even tolerable, and that claim is based on…what exactly?

The standard explanation of this rigid attitude is that observed male-female differences are "socially constructed," that is, they occur only because females behave as they are expected to behave. But, again, how do we know this? What research is it based on? Once more, there is none. The campus feminist orthodoxy says essentially: Don't bother us about research; we know what the truth is, and we have the right to *demand* that you accept our version of truth or we'll punish you; and no, don't even dare to ask us how we can back it up. If the old academic world were still with us, the response to all of this would certainly be: Don't be ridiculous; we don't let unsupported speculation get the status of unassailable truth as easily as that.

The defense of such a logically absurd position is unashamedly political. Allowing the question to be discussed is thought to impede the progress of women in the workplace by giving employers an excuse to discriminate against female applicants for jobs. But this is patently nonsense: in the real world, employers everywhere are desperate to find qualified women for STEM jobs, and that reality shows no signs of going away any time soon.

Campus radical feminists don't care one bit about the well-established fact that academia is a place that exists precisely in order to search for the truth regardless of any other considerations, and especially regardless of political considerations. In this instance, pigheaded political intransigence keeps a fascinating subject for research walled off from open discussion on campus. Yet it is one that will never go away. When a species has two forms that differ significantly in size, in physical strength, and in the part they play in reproduction, and when it is well known that these major differences are in turn related to all kinds of further physiological differences, it would be rather odd if no differences of temperament or aptitude accompanied these primary differences. Is male incarceration at rates that dwarf female incarceration just an accident? Is less risk taking by females unrelated to the extent of their physical strength? There may be no need to commit ourselves too quickly to answers, but there is no reason to accept that we may not ask the questions. The campus as an institution owes us thought and evidence on contentious questions of the day—not a concerted attempt to stop anyone from asking those questions by screaming at them and labeling them sexists and fascists.

The campus orthodoxy on this issue not only rests on absolutely no evidence, but actually flies in the face of mountains of well-known evidence to the contrary. Steven Rhoads surveyed that evidence in his book *Taking Sex Differences Seriously*, where he showed that there is overwhelming evidence of significant differences of temperament, interest, and abilities between men and women.[3] And yet campus ideologues engineered the dismissal of a president of Harvard University not even for saying there *are* such differences, but just for saying that there *might* be. Apparently, on campus you must now accept and assert what almost everyone knows to be a lie in order to please the ideologues, or you can lose your job. If you want to pursue this fascinating subject, you must make sure to do it somewhere else.

Nothing could show more convincingly that when we allow politics to reign on campus, honesty and integrity are crushed, and the academy becomes its polar opposite. The place where careful empirical research used to be conducted to help resolve difficult issues in the wider world becomes instead the place where the most extreme and divisive approaches to those issues silence all alternatives. Instead of doing something useful for society by spreading enlightenment on contentious issues, the academy does the opposite—it spreads falsehood and bigotry. Far from being the place where careful thought provides well-considered answers to important questions, it's now the only place where you may not even be allowed to ask the questions.

. . .

Now let's look at a second way in which the modern campus has to a large extent abandoned something that had always been regarded as one of its most basic functions. The society in which we live is built on the thought, writings, and investigations of a large number of remarkably insightful and gifted people over many centuries and in many different countries. The repository of this accumulated thought and knowledge has been academia. One of the main reasons that students go to a university is to be introduced to this great storehouse of knowledge. As I've already argued in Chapter Four, a grounding in at least some of this material is essential to an education for citizenship. But there is more to it than that. As the storehouse of knowledge, academia represents the present state of thought on matters large and small. New thinking must always take place in the context of all that is currently known on any given topic. Mastery of the present state of affairs is a first step to breaking new ground. Isaac Newton famously said that if he saw far, it was because he stood on the shoulders of giants. Students too can stand on the shoulders of giants by going to college. And first-rate academic teachers help them get up to speed on where thought and knowledge now stand.

A university education might involve many things, but immersion in the record of prior thought in particular areas of knowledge has always been an important part of it. Yet this essential feature of a university education is now being neglected in many areas of knowledge. Why? The answer is that this way of proceeding required a respect for what we have inherited from our past, and for those who laid it down for us—in other words, a reverence for the greatest of our predecessors. But the temperament of campus radical activists does not incline them to that kind of reverence. They don't look at our past and see opportunities to learn from the outstanding thinkers and researchers who have bequeathed so much to us, but instead see only a history of racism, sexism, and greed (and so on) that must be overcome in order to build their imagined utopia. Their attention is not on what they think of as the blighted past; the only kind of wisdom they care about is their own schemes for reshaping the future of our society. Students who enter college thinking that they will get an education in the vast knowledge that has been handed down to us will find themselves instead pushed straightaway into an ill-informed version of present-day radical politics.

The radicals' obsession with the present and its progress toward a transformed future inevitably means that they never understand their own place in the history of ideas. They think of themselves as anti-Western, but if they understood where their beliefs came from they'd know that those ideas are all very Western ideas, the thinkers who developed them being solidly part of the Western tradition. Radical egalitarianism is based on the ideas of Western thinkers; the abolition of the worldwide practice of slavery was a European cause and achievement; equal rights for women were fought for and attained in the West; and it was the European Enlightenment that led to the end of empires. Properly understood, the place in the spectrum of political ideas that campus political radicalism occupies is that of an uncompromising but confused Western extremist. If we want to examine the history of the radical left, there is only one place to find its origins: within the Western tradition.

Be that as it may, the fact remains that we now have a willed ignorance of what has been handed down to us—the legacy of recorded thought, and the lessons to be learned from the salient events in the history of our civilization. The great irony here is that students badly need to become acquainted with the sources of the ideas of faculty radicals, and with how poorly they have fared whenever they have been implemented. As Santayana famously said in 1905, "Those who cannot remember the past are condemned to repeat it." If we were to let campus radicals lead us into their brave new world, we and they would have to learn the lessons of history all over again. Radicals evidently don't want us to learn those lessons from history, and at least some of them certainly know that we would learn how badly their ideas have worked out in the past.

What is it that is replacing an education in the great storehouse of accumulated knowledge of our civilization on the radicalized campus? A recent study by UCLA's Higher Education Research Institute gives us the answer.[4] It found that more faculty now believe that they should teach their students to be agents of social change than believe that it is important to teach them the classics of Western civilization. In academia, of all places, a vital academic goal now ranks below a political one, in spite of the fact that almost every college and university is governed by statutes and bylaws that require them to be kept free of political influence.

• • •

There is a third way in which academia has abandoned one of its most important contributions to society. It used to provide a valuable service by framing issues in a context broader than the one from which they immediately arose. An issue that looks a certain way in the narrow context of present-day political controversies might look very different when placed in a wider context, often a historical context. We understand something happening in our own time far better if we know how it developed. And, indeed, much of the stunning foolishness that we now see on the campus originates in a failure to summon up the wider historical context that we used to get from academic scholars.

Take an easy example, concerning a theme we looked at a little earlier: On campus right now, any discrepancies in the representation of women relative to men in the workplace, or differences in rates of pay between the sexes, are reflexively attributed to a patriarchal plot of long standing, one that women are only now escaping from. But if we simply do what academics always used to do—set the matter in broader historical context—this explanation is soon shown to be complete nonsense, because profound changes in human life during the last few centuries have given women opportunities that they could not possibly have had before.

The changes in question are of many kinds: medical, technological, and social. Before modern medicine, a woman would need to have a large number of children to be sure of raising two or three to maturity, since many would probably die before reaching adulthood. Before modern contraception, she would likely be having children one after another in any case. And before the welfare state, everyone would need children to look after them in old age, so having children was the equivalent of social security. It was not the kind of free choice it is today. In former times, therefore, bearing a large number of children was likely to take a very large bite out of a woman's lifespan, which was typically much shorter than it is now. It would simply not be realistic to think that in premodern times the average woman's chance of a modern kind of career could have been what it is at present.

Technology has made a huge difference here. Easy travel by automobile gives women flexibility that makes family needs much less of an obstacle to a career than they once were. In earlier times, it was dangerous enough for a man to travel alone between one town and another, but for a woman it would have been madness. Today, well-policed highways make it a different story. At the same time, electrical energy makes the differences in physical strength between men and women far less important. A woman couldn't swing an axe to the same effect as a man, but she can now throw a switch or operate heavy power equipment just as easily. Taken together, these differences in historical context mean that career opportunities for women in the past could not possibly have been what they are today.

If the academy were still functioning normally, the rigid dogmas of historically illiterate radical feminists would be set in proper historical context by competent historians, and we should then be done with them. The academy used to be a place where reason and evidence were decisive, and where foolish ahistorical ideas could never compete with more realistic ones. Yet sadly, academia itself is now the origin and the stronghold of ideas based on contextual ignorance. Campus radical feminists will never let the facts of history get in the way of their ritual denunciations of the perennial patriarchal plot against women.

To be sure, there is nothing wrong with a debate about the extent to which the historical circumstances I've mentioned should or should not modify the position taken by the "evil patriarchy" school of thought. Anything and everything can and should be questioned on a properly functioning university campus—it's the academic way. But it's not the campus feminists' way, as the shouting down of Christina Hoff Sommers demonstrated. Any attempt to bring to light something that might reduce the justification for radical feminist rage is forbidden. This is behavior unworthy of university faculty, yet on campus nobody does anything to stop it.

We should all be grateful to those scientists, engineers, inventors, and medical researchers who brought about the changes that freed women from the restrictions that in the past kept them from doing what they now so much enjoy doing. But campus radical feminists won't give thanks to them, because doing so would destroy the narrative they love so much. For them, evil patriarchy is not a theory to debate, it's a given, and that's all there is to it.

When politicized professors abandon the habit of setting issues in a wider historical context to understand and elucidate them, they can say ridiculous things. As we've seen in an earlier chapter, they can fixate on an anachronistic search for racism on every page of American history when serious attention to historical context would put things in an entirely different light. But surely the most important historical context that campus radicals miss is the way in which modern life developed in the last two hundred years, and in particular where its defining innovations came from. They talk accusingly of "white privilege," meaning that whites have unearned advantages which they enjoy at the expense of others, and "cultural imperialism," meaning that whites disparage other cultures when they try to make everyone else read and study aspects of their culture. But in using those terms as they do, the radicals show again that they completely misunderstand the historical situation that they are in.

Throughout human history, major innovations have from time to time changed the way people lived. The inventions of the wheel and of agriculture are obvious examples. Those innovations had to start somewhere, among particular groups of people, and this means that the living standard of the innovators would suddenly advance beyond that of their neighbors. Naturally, the inequality in levels of development would soon vanish as the innovations spread to those neighbors.

Were other groups resentful about the "wheel people privilege" of the culture that first had the wheel? Did they resent the "cultural imperialism" of the innovators as they felt compelled to adopt the wheel themselves? It's not too likely. They probably just got on with enjoying the advantages of the wheel; it would have been foolish not to. Complaining about the innovators whose inventions have benefited them so much would be absurd—but that is what present-day campus radicals essentially do with their complaints about "white privilege" and "cultural imperialism."

The historical context of "white privilege" that must be understood is this: of all the innovations that have propelled human life forward, none have been so complex or far-reaching as the accelerating growth of science and technology since the late eighteenth century. And it is still unfolding. Change had come slowly for millennia, but suddenly it went into high gear. Rapid progress in scientific knowledge and technology led to the industrial revolution (including the steam engine, railways, and the internal combustion engine), electrical energy, modern medicine, and much more besides. These developments promptly began to change human life dramatically: average lifespans have now more than doubled; diseases that once devastated entire countries have been tamed; populations that were always on the verge of severe hunger became well fed; economies grew so strong that many now live as only a privileged elite did in the past; literacy became universal instead of being enjoyed only by very few; people who once would never have ventured beyond a small area could now travel widely and experience other cultures; individuals thousands of miles apart could communicate easily, and a great variety of entertainment and information became freely available to anyone through television and then the internet. Democratic government spread, and ease of travel led to a sense of a common humanity in place of the formerly ubiquitous tribalism.

But as always, this giant leap forward in human civilization had to begin somewhere, and in this case it was mainly among western Europeans and their North American cousins. Individual strands that fed into it came from other times and places, but this was where everything suddenly came together to set in motion the most profound change in human life that history has ever seen. It has already spread well beyond the innovators: lifespans have increased everywhere in the world, and European technology is now widely used.

Since this change started among Europeans, it is not surprising that they enjoyed its benefits first or that something of that initial advantage still lingers today. To call this "white privilege" is silly. It was neither unearned for the group that after all launched the changes, nor was it gained at the expense of others. On the contrary, other groups benefited as the innovations spread to them. History tells us that the initial gap that opens up between innovators and everyone else will close sooner or later. It has almost closed already as far as life expectancy is concerned. And, of course, nobody can know where the next major innovation in human life will come from.

Some minority groups complain when their traditional clothing is "appropriated" by Europeans, but those same people routinely visit dentists, board trains, switch on electric lights, and use iPhones—all of which constitutes a far greater "cultural appropriation" than the one they complain of. Even making the charge of "racism!" appropriates the Enlightenment values that began in Europe and conquered tribalism.

The accusations of "white privilege" and "cultural appropriation" are silly enough, but the fixation on "cultural imperialism" does real damage. For when a major civilizational advance takes place, the way forward for those outside the innovator group is clear: it is by assimilating the innovation and moving forward armed for better things. To judge by the disproportionately large numbers that get admitted to the University of California at Berkeley, Asian American students are not letting the silliness about "cultural imperialism" stop them from getting ahead. But the progress of other minority groups is being sabotaged by calls to resent the innovator group because of the temporary advantage that its culture's far-reaching innovations gave it.

It doesn't matter which group led the way to modernity, when it will soon belong to everybody. Only one group thinks otherwise: the angry political radicals who are at war with their own society's success. Their political agenda and ideology compel them to disparage it, and so they try to get minority students to believe that mastering the thought and knowledge that played a large part in the development of modern life pays homage to some dead white males. But if you want to master modern life, you must read those who shaped it—those who led the way out of the formerly ubiquitous tribalism that radicals seem determined to lead us back into.

It's true that Europeans thought rather well of themselves as their scientific and technological revolution started to put some distance between themselves and cultures that did not initially take part in it. But given the large discrepancy that suddenly arose between the levels of development of different societies, it was the most natural thing in the world that those who were leading the way to modernity would at first think of those who lagged behind as less accomplished than themselves. And it's equally natural that this state of affairs would not last very long.

Why do the people who run our campuses consistently ignore the objections to what they say about American society that are suggested by even the most cursory look at historical context? The answer is probably that while *they* don't like their own country's success, they know that it's enormously influential on the world stage, and so they are driven to look for ways to cut it down to size. When they see anything that might be an opportunity to do it, they don't stop to make sure that it really makes sense. And the result is that they consistently end up saying things that are absurd. Their embrace of cultural relativism is certainly a case in point: they don't seem to notice that it commits them to judging North Korea to be no worse than America. Robert Edgerton wrote an entire book on cultural relativism entitled *Sick Societies* in which he showed how appalling life can be in many of the societies on this earth.[5] In the real world beyond the campus, there really are many societies that even campus radicals would not want to live in.

The campus radical always faces a dilemma: if he wants to find fault with his own society, he has to invoke universal standards by which to judge it. But if he wants to cut America down to the size of all other cultures by appealing to cultural relativism, he has to abandon universal standards of judgment. You can hold one of those positions, but not both. The most discouraging thing about the modern campus is that people who hold professorial appointments, no less, don't care one bit about this elementary self-contradiction. Anyone who points to it is ignored. Never have academics had such contempt for the logic of arguments.

Just as radical faculty use cultural relativism in an attempt to undermine the achievements of Western society, they use the "postmodern" notion that there is no such thing as truth to undermine Western knowledge and wisdom. But that only entangles them in the same kind of self-contradiction that cultural relativism got them into. If there is no truth, then America is diminished, because the solidity of modern scientific knowledge is so central to its way of life. But radicals show us that they don't really believe what they are saying. How do we know this? Because anyone who dares to express an idea that they disagree with will soon find that these allegedly sophisticated postmodernist skeptics vehemently insist that they are right and everyone else is wrong. They might even back up that insistence with a shout-down. In other words, *you* don't have a right to appeal to truth, but *they* do, and they won't even allow you to speak if you challenge one of their sacred cows. Truth for me but not for thee.

. . .

On top of all this, there is a yet more important change in the way the university now functions, and that is in the everyday character of life on the campuses. It has altered beyond recognition. A college campus used to be notable for the presence of people who were more than usually thoughtful, who expressed themselves carefully and listened respectfully to others. Respect for rational argument wasn't just a matter of politeness; everyone knew that if you wanted to advance knowledge you had to learn as much as you could from others. Open-mindedness was more than a virtue—it was a necessity. Even opinions that seemed eccentric at first glance might turn out be the source of breakthroughs in knowledge. We couldn't afford to shut anything out by shouting it down. Too much might be lost that way.

For anyone who still preserves a memory of what that kind of flourishing, well-functioning academic community felt like, the current state of campus life is heartbreaking. The closed-mindedness and bullying ways of political radicals make serious discussion of social and political issues virtually impossible. The intellectual curiosity that used to be the basis of campus life is not just made unwelcome, but treated as dangerous.

The trouble is that radical politics at its core is both emphatic and exclusionary. It *demands* to be accepted as the position that sweeps the board, and that is why it always wants to silence disagreement. Careful analysis of issues would teach students the art of thinking independently, but that's of no use to radicals: they know exactly what they want. If radical activists had to compete on equal terms in a marketplace of ideas ruled by precise reasoning and carefully assembled evidence, they would lose. Accordingly, they must make sure that can't happen. Daniel J. McLaughlin explains how this works with respect to students: "Activists take advantage of a youthful fervor combined with youthful ignorance and overconfidence to promote their own agenda, not to develop reasonable citizens well educated on the issues."[6] The ignorance of the young, instead of being corrected, is now exploited.

The enforcement of radical orthodoxy on campus is frequently quite vicious. Even small deviations are hunted down and punished. Take the incident from 2018 in which a University of Georgia professor, Charles Davis, tweeted congratulations to a childhood friend, Brian Kemp, who had just become the Republican candidate for governor of his state. Davis was denounced as a racist for no other reason than that he was friendly with a Republican. The attacks seem to have broken his spirit, as he eventually issued a groveling apology—one so disgracefully abject that he actually praised his meanspirited, narrowminded attackers: "I'd like to apologize to anyone offended by my tweet shout out to Brian Kemp. It was ill-timed and poorly written. I've read and learned so much from you all and will endeavor to be more thoughtful."[7] What he had really learned, of course, was that campus radicals are so full of spite that life becomes intolerable if they come after you, however trumped-up their reason. Something that the Weinsteins at Evergreen, the Christakises at Yale, and a host of others had similarly learned.

Another event of the same kind occurred when Marc Short, who had been legislative director in the Trump administration, was offered an appointment at the Miller Center of the University of Virginia. The Miller Center specializes in studies of the presidency and public policy. An appointment like this might sound rather routine: having a person with experience at the very center of a presidential administration is what one might expect of the Miller Center. In any case, Short would be just one conservative voice among hundreds to the left in the modern university. But the result, again, was violent hatred. A petition opposing the appointment was signed by two thousand members of the campus community. Two thousand signatories is not about logic, it's about bullying. One faculty member pronounced that "Short's hiring is an institutional and moral crisis" because "the Trump presidency does not represent American democracy and has upended the political order." She did not explain how an elected president does not represent American democracy—surely that's exactly what it does represent. As the historian John Rosenberg suggested, the appropriate word for this is McCarthyism.[8] Will we soon see hearings with the question: "Do you now or have you ever worked for Donald Trump?"

One has to wonder why the campus atmosphere has become so poisonous that Charles Davis felt forced to make an obsequious apology reminiscent of public confessions at a Soviet show trial, and so childish that grown men and women throw a temper tantrum at the prospect of having a single Republican added to a University of Virginia faculty that is so safely tilted far to the left. These are people who complain all the time about hate speech, yet their own hatred of anyone who disagrees with them is completely out of control. The modern campus seems more like the Salem of old than an institution of higher learning. On campus you may admit to being a member of all kinds of fringe political parties (Green, Peace and Freedom, etc.) that have barely any credibility off campus, but you may not admit to having any sympathy with one of the two major, enduring political parties in the life of the nation. If you do, your social life on campus will be over, and you will probably be vilified.

Anyone from the outside world who has spent a reasonable amount of time on the politically radicalized campus will likely have been struck by how simplistic and static are campus discussions of political and social matters. It's over 150 years since publication of the first volume of Marx's *Das Kapital*, and it would be surprising if a theory that was formulated during the early stages of the industrial revolution were not in need of considerable revision in light of all that has happened since then. But the world of campus radicalism is still infatuated with those ideas. There are far more courses on Marx than any other political philosopher on today's campuses. They are places of ideological suspended animation, with the dominant faction stuck in political adolescence.

Most political topics are fairly complex, and solutions that manage to deal with all the ramifications of any given social problem in a reasonably complete way have always been hard to find. For example: how do you run a humane welfare system so that nobody starves, without creating more poverty by luring people into relying on government handouts? That kind of difficult, fundamental question has occupied theorists for hundreds of years, and there are many more like it. But all the conversations I overheard in the corridors of the radical campus framed the matter in starkly simplistic terms. Solutions were easy: all you had to do was force the greedy rich to part with their money so that it could be given to those who didn't have it. Across a range of social issues that need careful thought and painstaking analysis of potentially dangerous unintended consequences, the campus radical has but one answer: put right-minded people like us in charge, people who know that greed and other forms of nastiness among the privileged are the entire root of the matter, and we'll fix the problem right away. This is the thoughtless attitude that has brought disaster to so many. The fact that radicals think political problems have simple solutions without unintended consequences is what makes them so dangerous.[9]

This simple-mindedness leads us straight into another problem of the politicized campus: its tedium. The radical message is both rigid and uncomplicated. It entails a small number of fiercely held beliefs, and this means that the same conclusion is reached over and over again. Yet human experience is endlessly varied, and so the variety of themes and issues that crop up both in the record of history and in the great works of literature is immense. That is one reason why a university education was once such a mind-broadening experience. But because radicals are obsessed with finding and denouncing racism, sexism, and greed everywhere, they sharply reduce the great variety of human experience to those few issues, which themselves are further reduced by repetitive one-dimensional judgments. When that happens, the academy becomes a boring, monotonous place.

Perhaps this is why new categories of victims and new categories of offenses against them are constantly sought. New personal pronouns are invented so that failure to use them can create new opportunities for outrage. There are "microaggressions," offenses against other people that are hard to see with the naked eye (of which more below). This all seems to introduce a little more variety into the obsession with identity politics, but there is a price to be paid: the campus becomes even more of a laughingstock in the eyes of the public.

· · ·

How does this monotony affect the business of learning on campus? The tedium of similar rants endlessly repeated in the classrooms has produced yet another shocking result: students now spend very little time studying. That's an understandable response to the lack of substance in what the radical campus offers them. Formerly, it took considerable time and effort to study the highlights of the history and accomplishments of our Western civilization. People who took the old Stanford University freshman core course (Introduction to Western Civilization) always reported that they had to work all hours of the day to read everything they were asked to read. Yet most say that they would not have missed it. It's quite another story when students are subjected to the same old stereotyped thought processes over and over again: find a racist, a greedy capitalist, a sexist, a homophobe, and then denounce them! How are students to remain awake? Solid empirical research shows that they respond just as one might expect. They don't put much time or effort into this tedious enterprise.

A study by two University of California economists, Philip S. Babcock of UC Santa Barbara and Mindy Marks of UC Riverside, found that whereas the average student in 1961 did 24 hours of academic work outside class every week, that figure had dropped to only 14 hours by 2010.[10] Richard Arum and Josipa Roksa independently confirmed these findings; in fact, they found even fewer hours of study outside class. Students on average "report spending only 12 hours per week studying." Worse still, "37 percent of students report spending less than five hours per week preparing for their courses."[11]

These discouraging results have been confirmed yet again in a study specific to the University of California, whose four authors found a mean of 12.8 hours of study outside class. They also broke down the figures by subject area: 15.1 hours for physical sciences/engineering, 13.7

for biological sciences, 11.8 for the humanities, and 11.5 for social sciences.[12] Evidently, the more a departmental faculty approaches political uniformity, the less work its students do, for the obvious reason: there is much less content in their courses.

Arum and Roksa also researched the question of reading and writing requirements. They found that reading assignments were often so minimal that a third of students reported that they had not taken a single course in the prior semester that required at least forty pages of reading. Their general conclusion is that "If students are not being asked by their professors to read and write on a regular basis in their coursework it is hard to imagine how they will improve their capacity to master performance tasks—such as the CLA [Collegiate Learning Assessment]—that involve critical thinking, complex reasoning, and writing"[13] Yet Arum and Roksa write as if this were an unfortunate oversight, or just laziness on the part of those professors. It is not. The plain fact is that developing skill in reasoning is not what these teachers want. Making converts is. The two different goals conflict: if you teach someone to think for himself, he might not see things as you want him to.

Another disturbing dimension to this problem emerges when Arum and Roksa report that African American students study even less than other students outside class: they put in 10 hours a week on average, instead of the 12-hour average for all students. They are also less likely than white students to take courses with more than minimal writing requirements. There may be many reasons for this, but one of them is certainly the demoralizing racism-is-as-strong-as-ever message they hear from politically radical professors. Everyone who wants to see black students be upwardly mobile through higher education must find this result tragic. Once again, we should note who is standing in the way of black progress here: it is the radicals who profess to champion minority causes.

If hours of study are now half of what they formerly were, the reason must be that students see no need to do more. Careful thought about challenging books takes time, as does learning to write well, but absorbing a relatively straightforward political narrative does not. The simple message of radical politics is easily memorized and regurgitated for an exam. Putting in extra time to think more deeply would bring no benefit to students, and it might well result in a clash with their teachers.

More evidence of the sharp reduction in mental effort now expected of students can be found in college reading lists. For example, a number of University of California campuses recommend a book to all incoming freshmen for summer reading. This practice used to introduce the students to college-level work by giving them books that are classics of thought or of great writing. But the UC campuses now prescribe mainly books that address hot-button issues in present-day leftist politics, all of them written at a journalistic level, and with a distinctly one-sided political message. For example, *The Omnivore's Dilemma* by Michael Pollan is an attack on industrial agriculture. *The World Without Us* by Alan Weisman is a radical environmentalist's meditation on the harm that human beings do to the earth and to other species. *Enrique's Journey* by Sonia Nazario is an account of the trials of life in the United States for an illegal immigrant child from Honduras. *Why Are All the Black Kids Sitting Together in the Cafeteria?* by Beverly Tatum is a book on the racism encountered by black students. Taken by themselves as the single summer reading recommendation to large groups of students, these are very poor choices. They don't challenge students either by complexity of ideas or by excellence of writing; on both counts they are mediocre. This is not education—it is propagandizing. Every one of these books takes up the familiar themes of left-wing radicalism that we have seen over and over again: victimology, anticapitalism, illegal immigration, radical environmentalism.

Alas, there is yet another troubling aspect to the sharp reduction of student effort, for it has occurred precisely when college grades have soared. As Patrick Allitt remarked, in response to the study by Babcock and Marks, "It's never been easier to get an A, and it's never required so few hours' study!"[14] Those rising grades have also correlated with greatly reduced knowledge and thinking ability among college graduates, as measured by countless studies. So: the less work that students do and the less they learn, the better their grades! Only on the politicized campus.

. . .

Perhaps the most dispiriting thing about the campuses now is the sheer stupidity that is so frequently encountered there. We expect universities to operate at a high intellectual level, but now they are often conspicuous for exactly the opposite. Hiring that looks mainly for radical activist zeal rather than intellectual distinction has gradually dumbed down the professoriate, and it shows. The national press regularly brings us reports of the latest foolishness from the campuses. Sometimes it's only what a particularly dim professor has just said, but all too often it goes beyond an individual case of folly.

A particularly sad example is Critical Legal Studies, because this is an entire program of studies present on many campuses. It's based on the notion that the law is a means by which the haves exploit and keep down the have-nots. In this view, the law is a system of oppression and social control. In the real world beyond the campus, however, the rule of law protects the powerless, while its absence makes tyranny possible. Without the rule of law, ordinary people suffer. The record of human history shows that economies flourish only where the rule of law prevails. Preaching to students that our laws are a system of oppression is extraordinarily foolish. What is even more disheartening about Critical Legal Studies is that these programs are disproportionately taken by black law students. Yet again, black students end up shuttered away from mainstream thought in a place where there is much talk of victimization and racism but a great deal less in the way of genuine thought and analysis. This is yet one more way in which the education of black students is sacrificed to the fantasies of radical activists.

The latest absurdity to appear on the radical campus is the notion of microaggressions. For example, asking someone "Do you speak Spanish?" is deemed a microaggression, since it suggests that the person addressed is not a real American. If you say that you think the most qualified person should get the job, that is a microaggression hinting that minorities are now getting unfair advantages in hiring. If you say that America is a land of opportunity, you are committing a microaggression by slyly insinuating that those who are poor must be lazy and incompetent.

All of this is met with justified derision off campus, where it's seen as just the usual campus folly. But one might have hoped that this particular inanity was limited to a few dimwitted students or faculty. On the contrary, combatting microaggression is now nothing less than institutional policy in the University of California, where President Janet Napolitano wants all department chairs and deans to undergo racial sensitivity training that includes a grounding in microaggressions. For those readers who find it hard to believe that a major university could put its name to this extreme level of absurdity (and I would certainly sympathize with that reaction), I am providing a link to the official website of one of the campuses.[15]

We should note, however, that there is more to the microaggression fad than just foolishness. For it entails yet another form of the persistent vice of the politicized campus, which is censorship of any political expression that challenges the prevalent radicalism. To forbid any mention of opportunity in America would shut down one key idea of free-market economics. To forbid anyone saying that hiring should be done on merit alone essentially shuts down people who think that affirmative action damages those it promises to help. The theory of microaggression represents a campus shouting down of dissenting views by other means.

In this chapter I have argued that the campuses are now miserable caricatures of what they once were. On this subject, Dennis Prager quotes Steven Pinker, a professor at Harvard (and a liberal atheist), saying that American universities "are becoming laughing stocks of intolerance," aside from a few disciplines—natural sciences, mathematics, business. Prager goes on to emphasize how destructive this all is:

> If you send your children to a university, you are endangering both
> their mind and their character. There is a real chance they will be
> more intolerant and more foolish after college than they were when
> they entered college. When you attend an American university, you
> are taught to have contempt for America and its founders, to prefer
> socialism to capitalism, to divide human beings by race and ethnic-
> ity. You are taught to shut down those who differ with you, to not
> debate them. And you are taught to place feelings over reason—
> which is a guaranteed route to eventual evil.[16]

To add even further insult to injury, this precipitous decline in the quality of a university education has happened at exactly the time that it has become much more expensive. Over the past two decades, as David Rathmanner points out, "tuition at all types of colleges has more than doubled, and in some cases has more than tripled." This rate of increase "has greatly outpaced the inflation rate—by at least 3 times for most school types."[17] We now make it relatively easy for students to meet the immediate cash outlay of attending college with readily available loans, but this has the effect of diminishing the consumer's natural tendency to scrutinize the real value of what he is paying for. The result is that students are starting their working lives shouldering large debts that will take them many years to repay, while in many cases what they are getting for it is little more than a piece of paper—a diploma certainly, but without the skill and knowledge that such a diploma used to certify.

University teaching has been my life's work. I'd like to disagree with Prager's sweeping verdict. But I can't, because he's right.

CHAPTER 7

The Campus World of Lies and Deceit

The gulf between what higher education was always expected to be and what now really happens on campus is vast. But since what is happening is forbidden everywhere by statutes, institutional regulations, bylaws of governing boards, professional standards, and the common understanding of the public, the radical campus can't admit to what it is doing. The gap between the universal prohibition on using the colleges and universities to promote radical politics and what is actually being done can only be bridged by massive dishonesty. As a result, lies and deceit are now a way of life on our campuses.

That the campuses are now engaged in a crusade to promote radical politics is beyond question, yet it is always denied, and has been for at least twenty years. All kinds of people at all levels of the campus, from junior instructors to presidents, have denied what is going on, and the motives for the deceit have been various. The partisans themselves lie to make it possible for radical control to continue tightening. Others lie to cover up their complicity. Still others lie because they are terrified of offending the campus left, which can bring savage retribution. And some lie principally to avoid having to act decisively to stop what is happening, as is their duty. That prospect terrifies the cowardly senior administrators who understand that what is happening is very wrong, but know that standing up against it would cost them their jobs. I'll give some examples of these various kinds of deceitfulness.

• • •

The deceit begins with the partisans themselves. The political radicals know that they can't openly proclaim a political goal without breaking the law, and so they claim to be promoting "social justice." But they use that term as if its meaning were something that everyone can agree on. They want it to look like an appeal to common decency and fair play. It's a vague term, chosen so that it seems not to entail any particular political measures or intentions. Campus radicals use it almost everywhere, because they think it will justify their activities without being specific enough to violate laws or regulations.

Take three examples from different campuses of the University of California: At UC Berkeley, the mission statement of an entire department (social work) includes a statement that students must be committed to "advancing social justice." UC Riverside's labor studies program is also said to be about "alternative models for organizing for social justice." On the UC Santa Cruz campus, the mission statement of the sociology department gets only a little more specific. That department "considers how society is organized in relationship to a vision of a just, free, and equal society—a vision that may require fundamental social change." The term "social justice" has now become common throughout the campuses of the nation. It puts political motivation front and center without seeming to implicate any *particular* politics. But of course it does.

If "social justice" means only what is right and fair, it doesn't refer to any specific political arrangement or set of facts, and therefore it can't be used to justify a particular course of action. It would simply be a general judgment of approval, with no necessary connection to any particular measures that would need to be taken to bring about a desired result. Indeed, ever since Plato asked "what is justice?" there has been an increasingly complex discussion of what it is or should be—and Plato made it clear that a multifaceted discussion had already been going on for some time. There has never been a consensus view at any time during the very long history of this discussion. Yet those who march under the banner of "social justice" pretend that there is a common understanding, shared by all, when there plainly isn't.

If a rallying cry is to have any force, it must announce clearly what it's for and what it's against. In this case, it must tell us what is regarded as just or unjust. What, one might ask, is the point of adopting a rallying cry that doesn't make your cause clear but instead conceals what it's about?

But of course that's the point. The campus radicals who speak of social justice have a very clear sense of what it means for them: it means their radical political agenda of redistribution and a vastly increased role for government. But faculty radicals know very well that they can't openly proclaim that whole departments are committed to a divisive radical-left agenda, and so they use a bland phrase that sounds quite benign. It is meant to deceive.

To expose the fraud in a way that would be incontrovertible, all that's necessary is for a group of political conservatives to join in the happy campus chant and say that they too are all for social justice. If that phrase were really just a general exhortation to do what is right and fair, they would have just as much right to it as anyone else. The conservatives would of course have in mind a concept of justice and of the means for achieving it that differs from the leftist one. We can be quite sure that radicals would be furious that their catchphrase was being used by conservatives, and in their indignation they would be compelled to admit that they themselves have not simply been invoking a generally accepted concept of justice.

Thus the content that they had deliberately kept below the surface would become visible. *Of course* conservatives aren't for social justice, they would say, because conservatives are not for redistributive measures (welfare, universal health care, affirmative action hiring, etc.) paid for by high taxes (especially on the wealthy) to reduce the gap between rich and poor. And they are not anticapitalist. Conservatives might counter that high taxes stunt economic growth and make everyone poorer, that overly generous welfare promotes dependency and therefore more poverty, that government-run programs never work well because 9-to-5 bureaucrats don't put their heart and soul into what they are doing as people who are running their own businesses do. The question here is not which side has the better case; the point is that now there would be a genuine debate, in which serious issues of public policy are spelled out and analyzed, and concrete positions are taken by both sides in a meaningful exchange. By contrast, asserting a commitment to social justice without further specification means nothing—unless it really means a great deal more than what the phrase itself says. Which of course it does.

The two main reasons for the obfuscation are clear enough: first, most people will disagree with the radical program when it is fully spelled out; and second, obfuscation helps to avoid the charge that the university is being used for a political purpose. "Social justice" as used by campus radicals boils down to the conceptual swindle of a bait and switch. They sell the idea as something that sounds rather pleasant, but having sold it they switch to something else that would arouse immediate hostility if it had been honestly presented.

Most universities have a motto, often one in Latin, and many of these contain the word *veritas*: truth. The pursuit of truth was once what universities were all about, yet everywhere they now routinely deal in deceit. The deceitfulness of the phrase "social justice" is now fundamental to campus life.

•　•　•

Another source of organized, large-scale deceitfulness on campus is the radicals' heavy investment in the idea that racism and sexism are everywhere, on campus as well as off. But college campuses are now the most politically correct places on earth. If a genuine incident of racism or sexism ever does occur there, the campus goes into a frenzy, with an orgy of demonstrations, demands for more diversity offices, groveling apologies from administrators, and so on. This is great fun for radicals, but the trouble is that real opportunities for it are pitifully few. So a distinct category of deceitfulness arose: the exaggeration of both the frequency and the seriousness of incidents that supposedly demonstrate racism or sexism.

One example is rape statistics. An innocent newcomer to the campus scene might assume that low rates of rape on campus would make everyone happy. He'd be surprised to learn that it's the other way around. Campus radicals need things to denounce, and a "rape culture" would feed that need splendidly. If they can't find any such thing, they'll invent it. And they do so by using statistics that are so obviously bogus that nobody should ever have been taken in by them.

The most prominent attempt to create a sky-high rape figure for college campuses was a 1985 study by Mary Koss, who initiated the claim that one in four women on college campuses had been raped. Christina Hoff Sommers examined this study carefully in her 1994 book *Who Stole Feminism?*[1] Even Koss had admitted that her figure included *attempted* rapes, though that didn't prevent the widespread repetition of the idea that one in four had actually been raped. But the details of the study made it clear that this figure was not just somewhat inflated—it was absurd. Fully three-quarters of the women that Koss counted as rape victims said they did not feel they had been raped. Nearly half went back to the same males for further sexual encounters, something that surely could not happen in such numbers in the case of real rape. Koss was including as rape or attempted rape all kinds of encounters between men and women that turned out unhappily for a variety of reasons, thereby stretching those categories to include things that no reasonable person would include in them. The willful inflating of the numbers has only become sillier with time. Morning-after regrets, consensual encounters followed by a breakup, both individuals drunk, males who were insistent before eventually obtaining consent, clumsy embraces that went further than intended, or just simple miscommunication—sooner or later they were all put in the same category as the heinous crime of violent rape.

The "one in four" idea was only a radical feminist's fantasy. It was so soundly debunked in the early 1990s that its use dwindled, only to reappear more recently as if nobody had ever shown how baseless it was. Heather Mac Donald documents how prevalent these absurd figures still are on campus, and demolishes them yet again.[2] Mac Donald also points to the unreality in all of this. First, if the campuses really were so dangerous that one in four women is raped there, no woman in her right mind would go to college. Yet the facts of the situation are exactly the other way around: women now far outnumber men on the campuses. Mac Donald's most powerful point, however, was to note how colleges typically act in response to a credible charge of rape:

"They go into emergency mode." For example, a real rape was reported in Harvard Yard in August 2012, "sending shock waves throughout the campus." The whole Harvard campus went into a state of crisis. A student complained that Harvard was supposed to be safe, which prompted the acid comment from Mac Donald: "Apparently, she hadn't read the copious materials from the Harvard's Sexual Assault Bureaucracy insisting that campus rape was everywhere."[3]

Radical feminists are so determined to inflate the statistics that they even find a way to count low numbers of reported rape as yet more evidence of rape: supposedly the "rape culture" makes women frightened to report rape. There is a general principle in research: if the way you have designed a research program rules out any possibility of contrary evidence, your results are meaningless. University-trained people were once able to see through that kind of "heads I win / tails you lose" nonsense, but apparently no longer.

This gross mishandling of statistics shows that campus radicals have very different motives from the rest of us. We want to see lower numbers, but they want to see higher ones. Mac Donald cites the American Association of University Women commenting on the fact that 73 percent of college campuses with student enrollments over 250 students reported no rapes in 2015. A report of zero rapes on the great majority of campuses would be good news for any rational person, certainly. But not for the AAUW, which pronounced this report unacceptable.[4] Campus radicals don't want to face the reality that women's rights are more secure in our society than anywhere else in the world, for this flatly contradicts their message that this is a corrupt society in need of radical change. Accordingly, they manufacture facts to fit their purposes. But do they really believe what they are saying? We can be fairly sure that they don't. The debunking of that "one in four" figure has been going on essentially unanswered for thirty years. By this time, everyone concerned cannot fail to know what is wrong with it. But it's simply too useful for people who want to find as much fault with their society as they can—provided that their integrity doesn't matter to them.

Once again, one cannot help noticing the reversal of the role of the university vis-à-vis the wider society. In the past, wildly inaccurate claims would surface in the political melee of ordinary life off campus, and they would be corrected by the careful, fact-based research of academics. Now, it's the other way around. Ordinary people keep the common sense they were born with and immediately grasp the fact that the extreme claims for rape statistics sound ridiculous, while it's now the campus that is the source of the nonsense. The campus whips up hysteria, and it's left to the rest of the world to dispel it with fact and argument.

Much the same holds for matters of race. The huge and still-growing diversity bureaucracy needs to justify its existence by finding racism where it doesn't exist, and again the result is deceit. When protesters shut down lectures that promise to give convincing evidence that police overwhelmingly don't discriminate, those protesters are probably not doing so out of ignorance. They know that facts do indeed exist that will destroy their reckless sloganeering and race baiting on campus.

Because incidents of racial hatred on campus are few and far between but afford such welcome opportunities for orgies of self-righteousness, there has been an increasing incidence of fabricated racial incidents, that is, hoaxes. The temptation is simply too great. The title of an article by Jarrett Stepman tells the story: "Fabricating Hate Crimes Is a Byproduct of Victimhood Ideology on College Campuses."[5] Stepman explains why a student might perpetrate such a hoax: "For students seeking attention and accolades from peers on a modern college campus, it may make sense to create the false impression that you have become the victim of a hate crime or some other kind of oppression. This is especially true given how quickly the stories are exploited for political effect by social justice warriors and an eager media, regardless of whether the stories are actually true." Exhibitionism is a familiar human foible, and racial hatred hoaxes seem to be a new variety of it.

These hoaxes are now so common that the title of an article by Eddie Scarry in the *Washington Examiner* pronounced November 2018 to be "college hate crime hoax month."[6] Scarry reported a series of incidents on many different campuses in that month all having the same structure: a student reports racist graffiti but later is forced to admit to having been their author. The student had "tried to make himself the victim of his own hate crime." Scarry's general conclusion was that "Left-wing college students have a difficult time finding the racism they're certain permeates everything. And so they're brazenly inventing it themselves."

We can see bad faith in matters of race with particular clarity whenever anyone tries to find out the real extent of racial preferences in college admissions, and the consequences for the students concerned. If we look at this from the point of view of the traditional academic researcher, *of course* he or she would want to know exactly how these policies are being implemented, and what their results are. A genuine scholar would wish to know all the facts of graduation rates of preferentially admitted students in relation to other students, how big the typical gap in test scores is between the two groups, what kind of students are being denied admission through the preferential policy, and many other questions relevant to a judgment whether the policy is working well or not. And surely, one might think, campus administrators would also want to know exactly what they are achieving with the policies they support so strongly. Who doesn't want to find out whether what he is trying to do is working out or not?

But administrations everywhere fight tooth and nail to keep those figures out of the hands of researchers. They keep the large discrepancy in test scores between the races hidden, and likewise the low graduation rates of students admitted by racial preferences. They don't want anyone to know the damaging results of these policies, especially the harm they do to black students, because they would have a dreadful problem on their hands if word got out. So they invent transparently ridiculous excuses for not releasing the data. In all matters relating to affirmative action, the campus lives by deceit, because affirmative action could not survive without it. Since 2014, Harvard University has been in court defending itself against a suit that claims it discriminates against Asian American students in undergraduate admissions. Everyone knows that Harvard does indeed do just that. The students know it, the faculty knows it, the outside world knows it, and the administration knows it. But Harvard is denying it in court. Harvard is lying, and Harvard knows that everyone knows that it's lying. Preferences in admissions are something you must lie about because the consequences of admitting to what you are really doing are so frightening.

As we saw in Chapter One, deceit was also needed to prop up the campus orthodoxy when Amy Wax and her co-author recommended a list of actions that would help minorities get out of poverty. The list was almost boringly obvious: get married before you have children, stay away from crime and drugs, get educated, and so on. But she called these "bourgeois norms," and that incensed the radicals. To suggest that blacks adopt middle-class norms is to strike at the base of the belief system in which racism can be the only real source of minority distress. And so Wax was called a racist for saying things that everyone knew to be perfectly true. Once again, lies and deceit are employed to preserve the radical narrative, even when everyone knows them to be lies.

• • •

The most difficult thing for campus radicals to cover up is the huge gulf between the real knowledge that the traditional university dealt in—complex and intellectually demanding—and the radical campus orthodoxy, which is not at all difficult to grasp, since it consists only in a few very simple ideas, all of which are easy to question and rebut. Their response to this comparison, in which they are at a decided disadvantage, has been to develop a dense, almost impenetrable jargon that they claim to be so highly sophisticated that lesser mortals will have trouble understanding it. Here is a celebrated example:

> The move from a structuralist account in which capital is under-
> stood to structure social relations in relatively homologous ways
> to a view of hegemony in which power relations are subject to
> repetition, convergence, and rearticulation brought the question
> of temporality into the thinking of structure, and marked a shift
> from a form of Althusserian theory that takes structural totalities as
> theoretical objects to one in which the insights into the contingent
> possibility of structure inaugurate a renewed conception of hege-
> mony as bound up with the contingent sites and strategies of the
> rearticulation of power.[7]

This sentence won the fourth annual Bad Writing Contest (1998) sponsored by the journal *Philosophy and Literature*, but its author, Judith Butler, holds a prestigious named professorship at UC Berkeley.

Unfortunately for the radicals, this jargon is so absurd that nobody but campus insiders has ever been taken in by it. It is just too obviously flimflam, meant to cover up a poverty of thought. Alan Sokal, a professor of physics, decided to put this matter to a test. Was this just pretentious, vacuous verbiage cloaking a simple-minded orthodoxy, or something more? He composed an essay that was pure nonsense by design, making all sorts of idiotic claims overlaid with the trendy buzzwords and verbal tricks of "postmodern" jargon. The result was a hilarious parody of radical-left writing. Nevertheless, the journal *Social Text*, which is highly regarded among campus intellectuals, eagerly published the essay. Sokal then went public with the truth about the piece: it was deliberately absurd.[8] Evidently, radical intellectuals were so mired in their own self-created deceitfulness that they didn't notice any difference between Sokal's manufactured nonsense and their own entirely earnest variety. Sokal had shown convincingly that the pretentious postmodern style was meant to create the illusion of profundity where there was actually none.

More recently, three young academics have done again what Sokal did, but on a much larger scale. James Lindsay, Peter Boghossian, and Helen Pluckrose composed not one but twenty different hoax articles on what might loosely be termed "grievance studies," each one clothing outlandish absurdities in fashionable postmodern jargon. Seven were accepted for publication and appeared in a number of different journals. They were peer-reviewed by "experts" in the field, who again couldn't tell the difference between intentional absurdity and what currently passes for serious research essays on the present-day campus.[9] What the trio of authors had proved was first, that the Sokal incident was not an isolated case, and second, that the condition he had exposed was, if anything, even worse twenty years later. Let's be clear about what this means: a whole series of academic journals now publish articles that even so-called experts in the field cannot distinguish from ludicrous parodies.

Phillip Magness gets to the heart of the matter in commenting on these hoaxes: "The fabricated articles only advanced to publication because decades of lax standards have made academically fashionable nonsense—including other forms of fraudulent work—the norm for celebrated scholarship in several of the humanities and social sciences."[10] By any reasonable standard this material is nonsense, but in thoroughly corrupted university departments it counts as "celebrated scholarship." The discrepancy between the reality of what these articles really are and their embrace by people who now hold prestigious professorships in the humanities should really give us pause. We are paying the salaries of these foolish people and giving them professorial titles that were once marks of great intellectual distinction.

• • •

In this light, we shouldn't be surprised that student interest in humanities courses has been sharply declining everywhere over the last three decades. Course enrollments are down, numbers of students majoring in those fields are down, faculty numbers are down, and job opportunities for newly graduated humanities PhDs are down. Everyone knows why this is happening: students are voting with their feet. The tedious political harangues of campus radicals don't hold the attention of students as Shakespeare and Western civilization did. Dropping enrollments is a response to the worthlessness of what is going on. Yet the response from the universities has been yet another example of deceitfulness.

The details of these declines in enrollment are easily available on a dedicated website called Humanities Indicators, run by the American Academy of Arts and Sciences. "The humanities experienced a substantial decline in their share of all bachelor's degrees over the course of the 1970s and early 1980s," it tells us. The data on bachelor's degrees conferred show especially rapid declines in what are labeled "historical categories" of the humanities, specifically, "English language and literature, history, languages and literatures other than English, linguistics, classical studies, and philosophy." In 1967, their share of all bachelor's degrees conferred was 17 percent; in the mid-1990s it was down to slightly over 8 percent; and by 2015 it was about 5 percent, "the lowest level in records extending back to 1949." From 2012 to 2015, the number of degrees conferred in the historical categories declined by 17 percent, and in one year alone, from 2014 to 2015, it fell by 9 percent.[11]

Benjamin Schmidt, writing in the *Atlantic* in 2018, noted some astonishing declines in majors for particular fields: "History is down about 45 percent from its 2007 peak, while the number of English majors has fallen by nearly half since the late 1990s."[12] What's more, these fields had already suffered major declines before the periods that Schmidt was looking at.

When universities see very low and still-dropping student numbers in certain areas, their first thought is to move resources to other areas of the academy that now appear to have a greater need of them. And so in 2010, the State University of New York at Albany decided to eliminate French, Italian, Russian, and classics from its curriculum. In 2018, a University of Wisconsin campus (Stevens Point) proposed to eliminate more than a dozen majors, including English, history, philosophy, and political science.[13] These publicized cases are just a small part of the reassignment of resources that is continually going on as humanities enrollments keep declining. My own campus (UC Santa Cruz) is currently struggling with the fact that the engineering division (mainly computer engineering) has a huge share of undergraduate majors (about a quarter of the total) and an even larger share of graduate students (about one-third of the campus total) while humanities enrollments have dropped so far that the faculty-student ratio is obviously a great deal more generous than that of the engineering faculty.

This suggests that students can still recognize nonsense when they see it. And that poses a very real problem for the politicized campus: greatly reduced student numbers in the most politicized areas mean that the radicalized departments no longer deserve the numbers of faculty positions that they still have. But reallocating faculty positions away from those departments generates resistance on the part of the radicals who would be fired as a result. Anything that threatens to reduce the numbers and the power of the radicals won't have an easy passage.

The deceitful response to the humanities cuts was a campaign under the banner "Save the Humanities." It's an attractive flag to sail under, but nothing could have been more cynically dishonest. Campus political radicals have demolished the traditional humanities curriculum, and now, faced with a loss of money and faculty positions, they began to argue what sounded like the traditional case for the humanities, as if that kind of humanities program still existed. Having long since rejected that case in favor of a politically utilitarian one, they now dusted it off again: The humanities are not directly linked to career opportunities as things like computer science are, but they give us the trained minds of broadly educated people by affording us access to a rich legacy of outstanding writing and thought on philosophical, ethical, religious, social and political matters. That of course is the argument that comes to mind when the slogan "Save the Humanities" is used. But for campus radicals, it's a flag of convenience only, and a deeply dishonest one. They are trying to save themselves and their power base by pretending that they are teaching the traditional humanities, which in fact they loathe. They have always despised the arguments that they now use.

There was indeed a time when "Save the Humanities" would have been an appropriate cry, but that was years ago, when they were being dismantled in one department after another, to be replaced with the intellectual triviality of endlessly repetitive identity politics, while timid administrators looked on and did nothing.

• • •

The deceitfulness that is inevitable in the use of academia by political radicals to advance their agenda eventually draws almost everyone else on the campuses into it. Even those who are not directly involved join in the deception rather than confront the degradation of higher education that it was their duty to prevent.

The case of Ward Churchill is illustrative. He had been employed by the University of Colorado at Boulder for twenty-seven years when the general public learned in 2005 about an essay he had published online the day after the 9/11 terror attack, entitled "'Some People Push Back': On the Justice of Roosting Chickens." Churchill wrote that the thousands who suffered horrible deaths in the Twin Towers had been

busy braying, incessantly and self-importantly, into their cell phones, arranging power lunches and stock transactions, each of which translated, conveniently out of sight, mind and smelling distance, into the starved and rotting flesh of infants. If there was a better, more effective, or in fact any other way of visiting some penalty befitting their participation upon the little Eichmanns inhabiting the sterile sanctuary of the twin towers, I'd really be interested in hearing about it.

This shocked the public. Not because it was a radical-left opinion—people were used to hearing that on college campuses. What really caught people's attention was that Churchill took radical leftism to such extreme lengths that the result was both savagely cruel and extraordinarily stupid.

Members of the public must have been struck by the huge gulf between Ward Churchill and what they remembered of their own teachers. They would have recalled those teachers always pressing them to write more carefully, to think in a more disciplined way, to grow beyond the bad habits of the uneducated: reckless generalization, inflammatory language, question begging, bad inference, and more. Yet here they saw a man with the title of professor at a world-class university writing and speaking in a way that would have gotten them an F in a freshman class. Churchill's words sounded more like the incoherent ranting of a drunk in a bar than the careful speech and thought of their teachers. How, then, could this man possibly be a professor at a major university?

The spotlight on Churchill brought heightened attention to his academic work, with several other scholars lodging allegations of research misconduct including plagiarism and falsification. The University of Colorado conducted an investigation, and in 2007 the Board of Regents voted overwhelmingly to fire Churchill. He then filed a lawsuit, but the courts upheld the university's decision.

Any reasonable observer might ask: What took the university so long? Didn't anyone ever hear him speak like this before? Why did the campus lag behind the public in reacting so negatively to this incoherent nonsense? How could he have gotten tenure in the first place? The public could easily see that Ward Churchill should not be a professor at a serious university, yet he had been employed by the University of Colorado since 1978, had been a tenured professor since 1991 and department chair since 2002. He must have been heard uttering his characteristic gibberish by hundreds of faculty, staff, and students over a very long time. His record of teaching, writing, committee and administrative work must have been scrutinized many times, and certainly before he was granted tenure. *The university knew exactly who he was.* And he wasn't just tolerated on campus for all those years: he had thrived there. Not in spite of what he did, but because of it.

What changed? Only that the wider public heard what he said. In other words, he *and the campus* got caught. And this meant that he had to be fired, not for what he said, but because he had been heard saying it by the general public. That public had to be left with the impression that this was unacceptable on campus—a completely false impression, of course. When considering what it took to get the campus to act, Roger Kimball observed that "the melancholy side of the affair lay in the fact that the [public] scrutiny had to be enormous and unremitting."[14] That is what it took to get the university to remove Churchill from the faculty. Absent overwhelming public attention and anger, university officials don't give the stunning idiocy of professors like Ward Churchill a second thought.

When we examine this whole sequence of events we are left with one inescapable conclusion: there must be many more like Ward Churchill on that same campus, for otherwise he could never have gotten one promotion after another over nearly three decades. But the others didn't get caught—he did. When the university fired Churchill it was pretending that it didn't tolerate people like this, but that was in effect a lie. It had known about Churchill all along, had accepted his behavior as normal and frequently rewarded it—until the public heard him speak. And then it was suddenly shocked, shocked, like Captain Renault in *Casablanca.*

Had the University of Colorado really been serious about getting to the bottom of what Churchill's twenty-seven-year presence meant for the institution, it would have set up a committee of inquiry to examine how a hiring mistake of this magnitude could have been made and have taken so long to detect, in order to make sure that it could never happen again. And that committee would also have been charged with finding out if there were any more such mistakes on campus—more Ward

Churchills. It would have had to confront the fundamental question: have tests of competence and coherence now been completely replaced by a search for ideological conformity in those parts of the campus that have been colonized by radical political activism? But none of this happened, for the simple reason that the university already knew the answer to the question. It pretended that Churchill was a lamentable aberration and a lapse from the university's standards, but it knew perfectly well that he wasn't.

What was going on here was easy to grasp: the only thing that drove the university administration to act was fear. Most of the time it fears the anger of the radicals most of all, but on this occasion a fear of the public—its major funding source—temporarily trumped that fear. But there was no sign of a genuine concern for the integrity of the University of Colorado.

· · ·

In 2012, the California Association of Scholars (CAS) made the most concerted and determined challenge that I am aware of to the politicized campus when it submitted to the Regents of the University of California a report entitled *A Crisis of Competence: The Corrupting Effect of Political Activism in the University of California*, which I myself wrote, as president of CAS at the time.[15] The comprehensive seriousness of this challenge was soon matched by the sweeping deceitfulness of the response from all levels of the university. Since the University of California is without question the largest and most prestigious system of higher education in the world, we were raising a serious question that deserved an equally serious response, but it's no exaggeration to say that the record of corruption that we documented in our report was only augmented by the dishonesty of the university's reaction to it.

This became an amazing case study in how administrators of heavily politicized campuses desperately twist and turn, dissemble and prevaricate, and finally stonewall—all to avoid the horrible prospect of being forced to do their plain duty to restore the integrity of the university, which would of course mean facing the explosive anger of their radical professors. Senior administrators are paid very large salaries that dwarf those of ordinary professors in the university, yet it was clear throughout that they had only one thing on their minds: self-protection. So terrified were they at the prospect of having to fulfill their responsibility that they pretended not to see the overwhelming evidence we presented. But their behavior told us in a dozen ways that they knew well enough how powerful it was.

Reports of egregious classroom politicization had been surfacing for many years by the time the CAS report was written, and university spokesmen had developed a standard response: This is all hearsay and unrepresentative anecdotes. But it was never said that the incidents would be investigated.[†] It's as if the police received an account of a murder having taken place, and then pronounced it merely hearsay *without ever investigating whether anything had in fact happened.* It's perfectly justifiable to say that a report turned out to be just hearsay *after* you've looked into it. But when you are confronted with an account of improper behavior in many classrooms, why would anyone dismiss it before looking into whether it might be true? This consistent omission tells us that university administrators don't want to find out the truth, because it might be dangerous for them. Before the campus became so heavily politicized, any such allegations would have been conscientiously investigated, but no longer.

As I drafted the CAS report I was mindful of the way that university administrators were ducking their responsibility for quality control, and so I assembled a great deal of evidence from published sources and studies. Much of what I drew upon was actually taken from the university's own printed catalogs and documents. That, I thought, would make it impossible to trot out the tired old "hearsay and anecdotes" excuse yet again. But I underestimated the extent of the dishonesty of university spokesmen, because when the report was published, that was

---

† This was essentially the response to David Horowitz and Jacob Laksin, *The One-Party Campus* (New York: Crown Forum, 2009), a book that documented the politicizing of a very large number of classes on twelve of America's major campuses. By questioning whether those examples were representative, academia dodged the central issue that the authors had raised: how could there be so many such cases unless quality control had long since broken down? Whether or not they were a majority of courses was beside the point. The academic world thought it could dismiss any need for corrective action if the examples given by Horowitz and Laksin were unrepresentative, but they were not, nor was the argument valid in any case.

exactly what both faculty and administrative spokesmen said. They had evidently all agreed to tell the same lie.

Unfortunately for the university, too many influential people recognized that CAS had made a powerful case that needed to be answered. The national press weighed in: the *Wall Street Journal* published a long article in its influential opinion section by the distinguished journalist Peter Berkowitz, who expounded our case persuasively. The two most important newspapers in the state of California (the *Los Angeles Times* and the *San Jose Mercury News*) ran opinion pieces by my CAS colleague Charles Geshekter and myself based on the report. National and local radio covered the report in dozens of different interviews. The public was now awake and watching.

The university could have looked at the situation that it faced as an opportunity: the general public was clearly worried about the politicized campuses, and the university now had a chance to explain itself to the public. But it soon became clear that UC spokesmen had only one thought between them: how to wriggle out of this highly embarrassing situation.

The university decided to play for time and kick the can down the road until the public lost interest and went back to sleep again—a well-worn tactic used whenever any incident brought the excesses of the politicized campus to the attention of the public. The University of California president, Mark Yudof, told me that the systemwide Academic Senate would do a study of the report. Months went by. Suspecting that something underhanded was going on, I searched the Academic Senate website. A one-page comment by the Senate leadership was buried on an obscure page of the site. What Yudof had called a study turned out to be only a brief letter addressed to him, which he never passed on to us.

The UC Academic Senate "study" relied on a one-word judgment of the report, and yes, once again, that word was "anecdotes." The Senate had joined in the lie that the rest of the university had told from the very beginning. Not a single fact nor any argument from the report was set out in the letter, let alone rebutted. This was no study at all. Curiously, the letter went on to recite some of the university's procedures and policies that were designed to maintain integrity in faculty hires and in teaching, and it claimed that these institutional safeguards were sufficient in themselves to ensure that what CAS documented could never have happened. But had those procedures actually worked? We had set out a mountain of evidence to prove that they hadn't. The adequacy of procedural safeguards must be judged by results, and by that standard we had shown them to have failed. But the university carefully avoided the question whether the safeguards had worked or not. Worse yet, it skirted a problem that was glaringly obvious: those procedural safeguards were mostly in the hands of faculty committees. If the faculty had become politicized, the foxes would be guarding the chickens, and the safeguards would have become worthless. Events would soon prove beyond any doubt that this was indeed what had happened.

The Academic Senate's claim as to the unquestionable sufficiency of these institutional safeguards was in fact shamelessly audacious. The Senate adduced the same rules and policies we had cited in our report to demonstrate that what was happening at the University of California was *in violation of its own rules*. We had shown that the rules were being violated, and the university's reply was essentially that this could not be happening because the rules forbade it! This could well replace the celebrated definition of chutzpa in Leo Rosten's Yiddish dictionary. It was no wonder that President Yudof had kept this Senate response from CAS—he must have understood how pathetically inadequate it was.

We had already decided to break through the "anecdotes" defense by sending Yudof a letter that specifically cited eight major findings of fact from the CAS report, asking him to tell us in each case whether or not he was concerned by them. I'll cite those points as they were expressed in our letter, since they will give a good sense of what the CAS report had covered:

1. Does the rapidly growing political tilt of the campuses not bother you? (2 to 1 in 1969; 5 to 1 in 1999; 8 to 1 by the middle of the last decade, with UCB at 21 to 1 in the social sciences, and 49 to 1 in the junior ranks overall—the shape of the future campus.) If this is not a "monoculture," can you tell us what would count as one for you?

2. Are you concerned about a campus climate that can produce the travesty of the UCSC "teach-in" on the Iraq war where all ten speakers were on the same side?

3. What about departments of political science that virtually exclude one half of the spectrum of political ideas? If Mill's dictum ("he who knows only his own side of the case knows little of that") counts as "words to live by" for you, do you think the campuses at present live by them? Or do they instead "not, in any proper sense of the word, know the doctrine they themselves profess"—the part of our citation from Mill that you omit?

4. Are you not concerned that official campus catalogs print (even after administrative review) departmental mission statements that openly profess political goals?

5. Are you concerned that the political tilt is greatest exactly where programmatic concerns would require it to be least, especially in "education for citizenship"?

6. Do you worry about the bizarre (and politicized) curricular choices that result in graduates who are ignorant both of the history and political institutions of the society in which they live, and of its having been shaped by the great civilization of which it is a part? (Yes, the national study [cited in the CAS report] did include UC Berkeley and UCLA.)

7. Are you not disturbed about a campus climate in which UC police must be put on standby every time certain kinds of speakers are invited to campus?

8. Are you concerned that documented classroom abuses are found even in basic or required courses where the entire departmental faculty must have known what was happening?

9. Are you troubled by widespread public disapproval of the politicization at UC?

Yudof simply refused to address any of these legitimate queries. But it was always clear that both he and we knew that he couldn't answer them because he knew that we were right.

It was at this point in our negotiations with the University of California over the CAS report that an incident on the UCLA campus proved conclusively that everyone at UC had always known perfectly well that everything we said in our report was true, and that they had been lying about it.

Just as the CAS report was being published in 2012, two professors lodged a formal complaint about Professor David Shorter's using his classroom at UCLA to promote the movement to boycott Israel. This was the so-called BDS movement: Boycott, Divestment, Sanctions. The evidence of the abuse was incontrovertible, and it was definitely not anecdotal. This was a potentially high-profile case that could easily arouse the public and fatally undermine UC's defense against the CAS report. The university panicked.

Complaints like this one usually take months to settle as they wend their way through the committees that the rules for due process would require. But the university was anxious to dispose of the matter before the public realized what it meant, namely, that what the CAS report alleged was absolutely correct. It went into full damage-control mode. Moving with great haste, the chair of the UCLA Academic Senate ignored all the settled procedures for adjudicating such cases, and unilaterally ordered the chair of Shorter's department to stop this abuse immediately—something the Senate chair had no authority to do. It was obvious that the university was desperate to bury the Shorter case quickly, before it demolished UC's arguments in response to the CAS report.

This panicky action spoke volumes. The only possible reason for the panic was that university officials knew the CAS report was indeed a truthful picture of what the University of California had become. In his alarm, the UCLA Senate chair didn't understand that he was conceding our entire case by implication: he was betraying his awareness that Shorter's behavior was completely contrary to university rules and ethical standards.

Unfortunately for the university, Professor Shorter appealed to the UCLA faculty Committee on Academic Freedom. The committee, according to the rules, ought to have rebuked Shorter for what he was doing in his classroom. Instead, it rebuked the campus administration, and said *unanimously* that there was nothing wrong in Shorter's use of his class to promote his personal political cause. That's right: every single UCLA professor on the committee said that using the classroom to advance the professor's political agenda was fine with them. Since the Academic Freedom committee's membership was determined by a committee elected by the entire faculty, there could be no doubt that the committee's verdict had considerable faculty support.

At one blow, the UCLA Committee on Academic Freedom had destroyed both parts of the UC Academic Senate's defense against the CAS report. The university had tried to pretend that our evidence of routinely politicized classrooms was nothing more than anecdotes. The committee destroyed that defense by ruling that promoting political causes in class was now normal and acceptable faculty behavior as far as the faculty were concerned—not just in Shorter's classroom but in any classroom. The UCLA committee's decision proved that the University of California had lied when it said that there was no classroom politicization.

But the committee also destroyed UC's claim that adequate institutional safeguards were in place to make such politicization impossible. Its own action proved conclusively that one of those very safeguards, the Academic Freedom committee itself, was now firmly under the control of political radicals. That committee was supposed to be a watchdog whose job was to guarantee the integrity of the university, but it was now being used to do the exact opposite: to protect the political use of classrooms. Here too, the UCLA committee confirmed that CAS was correct and that the university had lied.

This incident also gave us a stunning demonstration of the extent of the radicals' power and of the administration's fear of them, because the UCLA Academic Senate chair who had first said that Shorter was clearly abusing his classroom now fell silent. He didn't dispute the committee's verdict, nor did he say that he had initially been wrong. Neither did he resign, even though one of his own faculty's committees had just repudiated him. Lacking the courage of his convictions, he just shut up.

The irony here was that by trying to bury the Shorter case in order to get themselves out of trouble, the administration was also trying to protect the radicals from exposure by CAS. That didn't matter to the committee's members, however. The radical faculty wouldn't accept any precedent that might limit their power to do as they liked in their class-rooms, and that fact was now completely out in the open and obvious to everyone, including UC's administrators.

Because the UCLA Committee on Academic Freedom had destroyed the basis for the UC Academic Senate's rejection of the CAS report, we wrote to President Yudof to suggest that since a committee with clear authority to speak for the entire UCLA faculty had gone on record as unanimously supporting an instructor's right to use his class to promote his political agenda, the UC response to us ("anecdotes" and "adequate institutional safeguards") was clearly false, and thus obsolete. It was now beyond any doubt that a controlling majority of the faculty saw classroom politicization as routine and legitimate, and that one of those much-vaunted institutional safeguards was now promoting it.

But instead of facing up to what could no longer be denied, Yudof put on a display of dodging and weaving that left his initial devious-ness and stonewalling in the dust. He is a trained lawyer, and yet he pretended that he didn't understand what we were saying to him. He told us that as systemwide president he could not intervene in a campus matter, but that wasn't what we were asking him to do. We patiently explained the point to him again: the UCLA committee's unanimous ruling proved that everything that CAS had alleged about routine politicization at UC was correct, and that the university's response was plainly false. As such, it clearly needed to be reconsidered. Yet again, Yudof tried to pretend he had not understood what we were saying: he argued that one classroom proved nothing. Of course he knew perfectly well that we were not talking about one classroom, but about what an elected faculty committee's unanimous ruling showed about the atti-tudes and behavior of the UCLA faculty, and about the corruption of the institutional safeguards that he had invoked.

We now told Yudof bluntly to stop pretending that he didn't under-stand what we were saying, and to stop dodging the question we were putting to him. Yudof replied that the correspondence had gone on long enough and that he was ending it. We should be clear about what had now happened: Yudof's inability to answer and his desperate evasive-ness had implicitly conceded that we were correct. His duty as UC's president was to safeguard the integrity of the university, but he repeatedly refused to do that; he seemed more concerned with safeguarding his job. Mark Yudof was paid about a million dollars a year in total compensation to maintain the university's excellence, and he continued drawing that magnificent salary even as he refused to do anything in this case to earn it. The radicals, for their part, at least believed in something other than themselves.

There was a pattern in all of the university's responses to CAS: President Yudof's wriggling out of questions he couldn't answer, the desperate effort to bury the embarrassing Shorter case, the stalling by promising a study that never happened, the hiding of the shameful Academic Senate response, the calculated dishonesty of the "anecdotes" defense—taken together, it all sent the unmistakable message that the university had no honest way of answering the CAS report, and so it resorted to a variety of dishonest ways. We can be quite sure that if any part of the CAS report had been unsound, university spokesmen would have pounced. That they didn't means that they couldn't. Without realizing it, they had paid us the compliment of admitting that they couldn't shake either our facts or the logic of our argument. They all knew that what was happening on campus could not be defended.

The governing board of the university, the Regents of the University of California, only continued this sorry tale of avoidance of duty. We had addressed our report to them because under state law they had the primary responsibility to see that the university was kept free of political involvement. In violation of her constitutional responsibility, the Regents' chair, Sherry Lansing, told us that she must defer to the Academic Senate's judgment. We now acquainted her with the provision of the California Constitution that requires an independent judgment by the Board of Regents. Lansing abandoned her first excuse for inaction and came up with another: the Regents, she said, had agreed that no further action be taken on the report. It was then our duty to acquaint her with yet another provision of state law: the Open Meeting Act, which required that all Board of Regents decisions be made at a public meeting. Even a series of one-on-one conversations by the chair with each regent would count as an illegal secret meeting under the law. We spelled out the point: since there had been no discussion of the issue at a public meeting, there had been no legitimate decision by the Regents. Lansing then changed her story yet again. Now she said that the Regents had never discussed the matter and were not going to—which flatly contradicted what she had said previously.

There had been a major story about the political corruption of the University of California in one of the most important national newspapers (the *Wall Street Journal*), and yet the Board of Regents couldn't be bothered to discuss or even to take note of the matter—even though keeping the university free of political corruption was their unique responsibility in state law. The Regents too are a part of this story of the lies and deceit that are rampant on the modern campus.[†]

I have dwelt on what happened in this one major group of state university campuses, but the culture of lies and deceit at the University of California is typical of the nationwide campus culture. What the campuses are doing is so far from what they should be doing that the gap can be filled only by misrepresenting what is going on, that is, by flagrant dishonesty.

[†] We should also note the lack of any intervention by the Board of Regents during the free-speech riots and mob rule on several UC campuses in 2017; this was yet another striking example of their lack of interest in ensuring the integrity of the university. Though public concern about these ugly incidents had reached a high pitch, the Regents stayed well away from the subject in their meetings. A reader of the minutes of board meetings around this time would get the impression that these incidents never happened.

CHAPTER 8

What Can Be Done to Restore Higher Education?

In this chapter we will consider what can be done about the breakdown of higher education that has been brought about by making it subservient to radical politics. But first let's make sure that we face squarely the full extent of the problem, and deal with a few common ways of trying to play down the seriousness of what is happening.

What have we found? Solid evidence that most students after four years on a college campus show no improvement either in ability to reason or in general knowledge; college faculties now virtually cleansed of all but left-leaning professors, and with the controlling faction being radical political activists who have neither the wish nor the ability to be genuinely academic thinkers and teachers; classrooms everywhere used for preaching the ideology of those political activists, not to teach students how to think for themselves—minds manipulated instead of minds opened; a campus atmosphere where a vicious intolerance for right-of-center opinion makes serious discussion of the issues of the day impossible; an extreme, destructive version of identity politics entrenched both in the faculty and in aggressive politicized bureaucracies; a climate of fear with respect to matters of political or social ideology throughout the campus; major damage to the prospects of upward mobility for minorities; a virtual end to teaching of the U.S. Constitution, and U.S. history no longer taught in a balanced and intelligent way but instead used to further the radicals' war against their own society; a dominant campus ideology that is irretrievably discredited by the misery it has brought wherever it has been tried; resistance to that ideology crippled both by the creation of a "cocoon of ignorance"[1] and by the silencing of contrary opinion; bitter, intolerant and ignorant hatred of the social and economic system that has made this nation the most successful in the history of the world; a determined attempt to end the kind of education that transmits the knowledge and wisdom of past generations; the nation's political climate poisoned by the hate-filled attitudes that many students absorb from radical professors; all of this sustained by a culture of deceit at every level of the campus; and students who remain strangers to any serious and well-informed discussions about social and political matters.

If we take all of this together it amounts to a national crisis of vast proportions. Excellence in higher education was one of the major reasons for this nation's success, but we are now living off the college education that was received by people who are age fifty and over. When this older cohort dies off, the nation will be largely without people who have been college-educated in any real sense. We simply cannot afford to let our college campuses remain corrupt to this degree. An advanced society like ours needs people who have had a genuine higher education, one that simply spending four years on a college campus does not at present guarantee. That is after all why we have long invested enormous sums of money and four years of our children's lives in it. At the present moment this huge investment of resources is not simply achieving nothing—it is being used for purposes that are highly damaging to us all. The kind of left-wing radicalism that has destroyed so many countries could achieve supremacy here too if indoctrination of college students is allowed to continue. We must act to stop this madness now.

Yet it's prudent to ask: is there anything that might be said to moderate the gloomy picture I've painted? Are there silver linings anywhere? And if so, exactly what hope might they give us? Let's look at some attempts to find remaining pockets of good in the situation.

·   ·   ·

The first attempt to give us hope comes from people who point out that it's still possible for students to find some worthwhile courses and some capable professors—the student simply has to look carefully and choose wisely. There is some truth in this argument, but on closer inspection we soon understand that it actually concedes almost everything. It draws support from the everyday notion that there is always good and bad everywhere, and that we are always called upon to exercise judgment in steering toward the good. But what is really being acknowledged here is that finding good courses and good professors is getting more difficult. If it's admitted that they are a distinct minority, it's also thereby admitted that more is corrupt than is not. This must mean that quality control has ceased to exist on the campuses, and if that is so, those remaining islands of integrity will further dwindle. As time goes by there will be fewer of them because the deterioration will continue until action is taken to stop it. The left/right ratio among faculty has been rising for fifty years, and the latest figures show that it is still climbing. Whenever an academically serious scholar retires, the replacement will almost certainly be a political radical. However bad things are now, they will be worse next year, and even worse the year after that, and so on.

With the rising numbers of radicals will come ever more outlandish politics, because Mill's principle tells us that the more politically unbalanced the faculty, the more extreme its political ideology will be. We are clearly seeing that principle at work: visiting speakers had been heckled for some time, but mob rule at Berkeley in 2017 was worse than anything seen hitherto. With even greater concentrations of radical-left faculty we can confidently predict that mob rule on campus will become even more spiteful and intolerant, and higher education will be dumbed down even more. And as political extremism further intensifies, the worsening atmosphere will cause attrition among faculty who would otherwise not yet retire. Good people will find the campuses more and more intolerable and will look for a less unpleasant place to work.

If, then, we want to find a ray of hope in the idea that there are still some good courses and professors, we'll have to face the fact that they are a dwindling asset and will eventually become negligible—unless something is done to stop the rot. Doing nothing amounts to complicity in further deterioration.

A second way of trying to minimize the extent of the disaster in higher education is to focus on STEM fields—science, technology, engineering, and mathematics. These will remain strong, it is said, because the radicals can't infiltrate and control them as they do the humanities and social sciences. But this too is unrealistic.

To begin with, every study of the political affiliations of college faculty shows that while STEM fields had for some time lagged behind others in the extent of their faculties' tilt to the left, they are rapidly catching up. The ratio in departments such as history and literature reached almost 100 percent two decades ago, while the overall campus ratio was about eight to one. Since the humanities ratios greatly exceeded the campus average, the STEM fields were obviously well below it at that time. The crux of the matter is this: though non-STEM fields reached virtual saturation by the radical left some two decades ago, the overall campus ratio has continued to rise steadily, and that must indicate an increasing leftward tilt of faculty in the STEM fields.

It might be argued that since the subject matter of STEM fields is not political, politics won't affect the quality of teaching and research. But sadly, the quality of these fields will indeed also decline with politicization. There are many reasons why this must be so.

First, the quality of a university department's faculty depends on the size of the applicant pools that it has to choose from. Universities are highly selective when it comes to faculty hires. It is always hard to find first-rate scholars in any field. While hundreds of candidates may apply for a professorial appointment, there are never more than a dozen or so who deserve serious consideration, and several institutions will be competing for them. The latest figures on the political affiliations of faculty show that STEM fields too are now beginning to appoint almost exclusively leftist faculty, which can only mean that they have greatly reduced the effective size of their applicant pools. With half of the political spectrum essentially excluded, there are fewer excellent scholars to choose from, and so the quality of teaching and research must certainly suffer from that fact alone. And if preference is going to a radical subset of the political left, then the size of the effective applicant pool will be further reduced, and the overall quality of STEM field appointees will be greatly inferior to what it formerly was.

But when radical politics wins complete dominance on campus, other factors will come into play that are certain to lower quality still more. For example, when a certain amount of the recruiters' attention in the process of selecting new faculty is on political congeniality, other factors, including intellectual quality, will be given correspondingly less attention. And when the preferred politics on campus is radical leftism, which militates against intellectual depth and complexity, such qualities will decline further. This is more than just a theoretical possibility, as a recent development in the University of California demonstrates.

On several of the UC campuses, applications for faculty positions must now include a diversity statement. Some campuses make such statements mandatory for promotions and merit increases as well. At UC Santa Cruz, for example, the campus requires "a diversity statement from any candidate being considered for a Senate faculty position, to allow evaluation of their past and potential contributions to enhancing and supporting diversity, equity, and inclusion. The statement should address the candidate's vision for contributing actively to diversity, equity, and inclusion at UC Santa Cruz through their research, teaching, and/or service. As relevant, the statement should also detail the candidate's past contributions through research, teaching, and/or service."[2] Some advertisements for faculty positions frankly announce that diversity statements take top priority. For instance, recent announcements for faculty jobs at UC Santa Cruz, including positions in biomedical sciences and computer science, have told applicants that "Initial screening of candidates will be based on statements of contributions to diversity, equity, and inclusion."[3] Thus, in the first cut for those positions, which will reduce many hundreds of applications to the small number to be seriously examined, the diversity statements will be the only thing that is looked at. Not professional qualifications in the field where the applicant would be teaching and researching. You could be a biochemist of Nobel Prize quality and you won't even get your foot in the door if you don't sound sufficiently jazzed about diversity. Apparently there is no limit to the folly of the radicals' diversity mania.

Villanova University has gone one step further: now the forms that students fill out at the end of a class to evaluate their professors are to include three questions on the instructor's sensitivity to issues of diversity.

These new diversity requirements will no doubt spread across the country until they are the norm in higher education. They will draw every single department on the campus, and every single member of the faculty, both new and continuing, into the destructive identity politics that rules the campus. Chemists and biologists will no longer be able to hide from it in their labs, because radical politics will have extended its tentacles into those labs too. By these means, the political commissars are strengthening their grip on the entire campus. If a scientist thinks that identity politics corrupts academic thought and teaching, he had better not say so.[4]

The process of corrupting STEM fields is well underway, as Heather Mac Donald has observed. On the effects of the diversity mania, she writes:

> The science-diversity charade wastes extraordinary amounts of time and money that could be going into basic research and its real-world application. If that were its only consequence, the cost would be high enough. But identity politics are now altering the standards for scientific competence and the way future scientists are trained. "Diversity" is now often an explicit job qualification in the STEM fields.[5]

If diversity statements are indeed to be a serious factor in judging applicants for STEM professorships, then people who are outstanding STEM academics will be passed over in favor of people who are less qualified, but more radical. In addition, many first-rate STEM academics will decide that they don't wish to take jobs in places under the control of people who are power-crazy and foolish enough to impose this regime on STEM fields.

Those fields will be further weakened by a general campus atmosphere that is repellent to talented STEM faculty. They have many more career options available to them than do faculty in the humanities. What always attracted them to college campuses was the pleasant prospect of living in a community devoted to intellectual pursuits. But campuses dominated by radical political activists and the irrational mobs that they inspire are highly unpleasant places. That kind of atmosphere won't attract first-rate STEM scholars so easily—and it may drive away many who are already on the faculty as the climate of intolerance and fear intensifies. Taken together, these factors add up to a truth that can be stated bluntly: to imagine that we will always be able to count on first-rate STEM work on thoroughly corrupted campuses is a pipe dream. The STEM fields will take longer to corrupt, but they will not forever remain intact as islands of integrity and quality in a sea of corruption. They are being drawn ever more into campus radical politics at this very moment, and that process will continue.[6]

Are there already signs of a decrease in the quality of teaching and research in STEM fields? Indeed there are. Many observers have begun to understand that much of the scientific research that is now being published is of doubtful value. A study published in 2018 by the National Association of Scholars has a title that spells the problem out: *The Irreproducibility Crisis in Modern Science.*[7] The assertions made in the study's executive summary will astonish people who still assume that science on the politicized campus remains uncorrupted: "Many supposedly scientific results cannot be reproduced reliably in subsequent investigations, and offer no trustworthy insight into the way the world works. In 2005, Dr. John Ioannidis argued, shockingly and persuasively, that most published research findings in his own field of medicine were false."

Clearly something has gone wrong with the peer-review process, which is supposed to guarantee that nothing unsound is published by first subjecting all new studies to scrutiny by experts in the field. Richard Smith (former editor of the *British Medical Journal*) did a little experiment that showed how badly peer review now works. He sent out a short paper to three hundred peer reviewers with eight serious mistakes in it. The result was: "No-one found more than five, the median was two, and 20 per cent didn't spot any."[8] If so many supposed experts in their field were so poorly equipped to see errors, what does this say about the general quality of research that is being greenlighted for publication? Smith comes to the shocking conclusion that "most of what is published in journals is just plain wrong or nonsense." He is talking about science, not the humanities! It isn't just occasional lapses; the *general* reliability of work in STEM fields is evidently now open to question in a way that was never the case in the past.

Beyond the erosion of quality in scholarship, is there a more direct effect of campus politicization on STEM departments? Can they actually become politicized? Indeed they can. Take the case of James Enstrom, an epidemiologist at UCLA who in 2010 was "indefinitely laid off" as a result of his research on the health effects of fine-particulate air pollution. In a large-scale study, Enstrom "found no increased mortality from exposure to small-particle air pollution that includes diesel engine fuel emissions." He proved that very expensive new air quality control measures were unnecessary, and that the studies on which they had been based were incompetent. Enstrom's work "exposed the truth about an activist scientific agenda that was not only based in fraud but violated California law," as one account put it.[9] For that, his departmental colleagues voted to terminate him after thirty-five years of service, declaring his research to be "not aligned with the academic mission of the Department." Translation: he told a truth that was politically inconvenient, and in so doing he made his colleagues and their support of needless environmental regulations look irrational. His conclusions were scientifically well supported, but politically incorrect.

It's clear that we cannot regard the STEM fields as eternally reliable islands of sanity within the politicized campus, nor see them as a mitigating factor when we are judging the overall health of the campuses. A genuine respect for the STEM fields should *increase* our sense that reform of the campuses is essential. If we value the contributions to society of university work in STEM fields, as we must, we should be deeply concerned about what is already beginning to happen to them, and even more so about their future. Instead of reassuring us, they give us yet another powerful reason to be alarmed about the state of higher education.

•   •   •

What can be done about this enormous national problem? Some measures that are commonly suggested will never work because they treat only symptoms, not the underlying disease. The Berkeley riots of 2017 left a deep impression on the public, and so it's not surprising that the most common approach to higher education reform focuses on new guidelines for free expression on the campuses that would spell out limitations on protests of visiting speakers. It's easy to understand the appeal of a measure designed to stop campus mobs from preventing the expression of opinions they don't like. But even if such a measure were successful in the narrow sense, we would not have touched the real problem. New campus regulations that pronounced the shouting down of speakers to be unacceptable would not do anything about the conditions that led to the shout-downs, specifically a faculty that is almost uniformly leftist and dominated by intolerant radicals. It wouldn't touch the classroom indoctrination or the encouragement of political hatreds. The teaching that leads students to regard certain legitimate political opinions as disgusting and intolerable would still go on. If you can't alter the routine political indoctrination that goes on in one-party classrooms, new rules for campus public spaces will accomplish very little.

We should in any case remember that campus administrations already have all the authority they ever needed to stop the shout-downs. Why should we think that new rules will get any more respect than the old ones did? Faculty will ignore them, as they do the existing rules; cowardly administrators will be no more likely to enforce them than they have been to enforce those already in place; and faculty watchdog committees will side with their radical colleagues whatever the rules say, as they already do. Neither new nor old rules will ever be enforced while radicals control all the enforcement mechanisms. Students will know that they can rely on leniency if they break the new rules, because they know that campus authorities are essentially on their side. At best, new policy statements on free speech might help in campus public spaces—though probably only with the aid of a heavy police presence—but will do nothing about the root cause of the problem: the ideological uniformity and extremism of the faculty.[10]

The prospects for the adoption of strengthened rules on campus free speech are in any case rather poor. The University of Chicago led the way in 2014 with a fine statement of principles that reasserted traditional ideas on the importance of unfettered debate on campus.[11] The statement emphasized that individuals are not free to make decisions on behalf of the whole community as to what can and cannot be discussed whenever they feel offended. This provision was obviously a response to a recent rash of shout-downs. The Chicago statement has been adopted by some fifty institutions, which might sound promising until we consider that the number that have refused to do so is in the thousands. The Academic Senate of my own campus, UC Santa Cruz, voted not to adopt the Chicago statement by an overwhelming margin. The Committee on Academic Freedom had recommended a "no" vote, having concluded that the statement was designed to protect the freedom of speech of conservatives, something which the campus naturally had no interest in doing.

It is sobering to reflect on the fact that the Chicago statement did no more than reaffirm understandings about academia that were virtually universal before the explosive growth of radicalism on campus, and yet approximately 99 percent of colleges and universities want nothing to do with it. Much the same happened with an earlier attempt to reaffirm commonly understood academic values, the "Academic Bill of Rights" that David Horowitz proposed in 2003. It too would have required that obstruction of speakers not be tolerated, that political considerations not be allowed to enter into faculty hiring, and that classrooms not be used for political indoctrination. But professors who had spent decades creating the radical campus on which they could shut down their opposition and use their classes to make political converts were not about to throw it away so easily.[12]

There is another commonly offered solution to campus political corruption that is equally pointless: it consists in attempts to persuade the radical faculty to see reason and do better. Many would-be reformers first explain how something particular that activist professors do is harmful to students, and then advise them not to do it, because their students aren't really learning when they do. These well-meaning reformers sound quite reasonable, as for example when Jonathan Haidt and Greg Lukianoff recommend that universities "rethink the skills and values they most want to impart to their incoming students," and suggest "a greater commitment to formal, public debate on campus." Why yes, that would all be so very sensible, as would their recommendation that "a shared vocabulary about reasoning…and the appropriate use of evidence...would facilitate critical thinking."[13] Surely, the politicized campuses should be grateful for such good advice. If only the faculty radicals had thought of this for themselves, the whole problem might never have arisen.

But Haidt and Lukianoff seem to have lost sight of the nature of the people they are dealing with. What they advocate is nothing more nor less than the kind of thinking that was commonplace in the universities before the radicals deliberately suppressed it; and they suppressed it precisely because that kind of thinking stood in their way. Haidt and Lukianoff speak as if the radicals, once reminded of the values of the real university, could just say: Gosh, we never thought of that; of course we'll do as you say. But they will never have the slightest interest in listening to what Haidt and Lukianoff recommend because they achieved control of the campuses by doing exactly the opposite.

This is not to deny that those who write trying to persuade the radical campus to improve its ways often characterize very well a particular aspect of what is crucially wrong with the campuses at the moment. Daniel McLaughlin, for example, summarizes one dimension of the problem accurately when he tells us that activists take advantage of the youthful ignorance and overconfidence of undergraduates to promote their own political agenda, not to educate them. If they think they are "empowering" young people by drawing them into political activism, McLaughlin suggests a better way: "teach people the skills that they can use to solve problems for themselves and for others and to understand and respond to reality in a way that actually gives good results. Help them to develop the intellectual and emotional maturity to search beyond the sound bites and easy answers to problems."[14] This is good advice, but McLaughlin too seems to have forgotten that campus radicals gained their iron grip on the campuses precisely so that students would *not* be empowered in this way.

Students are prone to rebellion but not yet mature enough to know what is worth rebelling against. Selfish radicals exploit this uncertainty to advance their own interests, and appeals to them to find a better way to develop the independence of students are rather beside the point. What we want of higher education is not what they want; radicals are not interested in teaching students to think for themselves. Advising them not to do exactly what they set out to do—and have done quite successfully—is a complete waste of time.

. . .

In years past I've certainly done my share of diagnosing what was going wrong and calling for the academy to change its direction.[15] But that was long ago, and the time for this is now well past. The problem of a corrupt higher education can't be effectively addressed until we focus on the essential core of the problem. We are only distracted and diverted from that if we are thinking about new regulations to guide the faculty, or seeking to advise them as to how academics ought to behave. The root of the problem is the character and temperament of present-day college faculty. Any solution that does not directly address and attempt to correct the problem of an overwhelmingly one-party, radical activist professoriate is no more than wishful thinking. *The problem is one of personnel*, not of rules or guidance. Large numbers of people holding professorial titles have neither any real interest in academic work, nor aptitude for it, nor the knowledge that would be required for it. The interests they instead have are completely incompatible with academic work, and fundamentally at odds with the nature of a university. Any proposal for real reform must take aim directly at this problem of a concentration of people who don't really belong in academia but are now numerous enough there to control it, to abuse it for their own selfish purposes, and effectively to destroy it. Because the campuses are controlled by the very people who are the source of the problem, they can no longer be reformed from within.

Some who have grasped this point have suggested that we should press the campuses to hire some conservative professors. In one sense, this completely misses the point, for what we really need is professors who don't politicize their classrooms in either direction. Suggestions like this also overlook the sheer scale of the problem: the preponderance of radical faculty is now so great that a few token appointees could not possibly make any serious change in what is happening on the campuses. A conservative appointment here and there could not even keep pace with the political cleansing that is ongoing as old-school retirees are replaced with radicals—the ideological imbalance would still be increasing all the time. Soon, nobody who doesn't already sympathize with the intolerant ruling ideology will want to be a part of the one-party campus anyway. Even some committed progressives, like Bret Weinstein at Evergreen State College, have left in disgust. With or without a few right-of-center faculty appointments, the great majority of the faculty would be creating a climate of hatred for ideas that get in the way of their political agenda. No meaningful change is possible while the radical faculty overwhelmingly control the campuses. Tinkering around the edges won't change anything. Token conservative faculty appointments, new free-speech policy statements, exhortations and advice for the faculty to behave as academics ought to behave—none of this comes to terms with the fact that the campuses are tightly controlled by large and well-organized coteries of radical faculty who are hostile to genuine higher education.

Academia cannot be cajoled or persuaded to return to a healthy state. Real change can happen in one way alone: by dismantling, as far as possible, the radical faculty regime. These powerful political clans will have to be broken up and removed. Nothing short of this could possibly restore excellence to higher education.

The first reaction to what I have just said is likely to be: That will never happen; so draconian a proposal is unrealistic; nobody will ever agree to it. And that might be true. But let us be clear: if we conclude that such a drastic course of action is too unrealistic even to consider, we will thereby have decided to live with the corrupt and destructive academy that we now have, because nothing else could possibly make any meaningful change. Radical activists have rebuilt the academy so that it serves their political purposes. It will continue to do so until we dismantle what they have constructed.

Anyone who is taken aback by the magnitude of this task should ask himself the crucial question: Do we really have any other choice? We spend enormous sums of money on what is supposed to be higher education for our young people, but the greater part of that vast expenditure is wasted, and those young people are wasting years of their lives too. Add to this the damage done to our society, which includes both the corruption of K–12 education by radical politics and serious damage to the political life of the nation by the spreading of a radical politics that loathes this country and its traditions. We can't go on deluding ourselves with the complacent thought that we can just muddle on because the college diplomas our children bring home look much the same as they always looked. We are paying a huge price for this delusion. We must face up to the fact that the institutions that resemble universities no longer are such in the true sense. We cannot do without higher education. We must restore our capacity to get it. We cannot let this charade go on.

No reform of any consequence can be made until the public sees clearly what has happened: the radical left, despairing of success at the ballot box, set out to infiltrate and eventually gain control of academia as an instrument to promote its political ideology; but using academia for a political purpose inevitably destroys it, as we have always known; and therefore restoring academia to health means *undoing* what the radical left has done—not tinkering with it or trying to control it with more rules. Nothing can be accomplished while what the radical left has created is still in place.

We must not succumb to the comforting thought that disarms so many when confronted with a crisis: that there are always cycles in human affairs, and we just happen to be at the bottom of one, but the wheel will turn again. The universities were splendid fifty years ago and they will be so again someday, this thinking goes. But this is an unwise and dangerous attitude. Ultimately, it serves to justify doing nothing. It tells us that we only need to wait for the problem to take care of itself. This is a misreading of history, and a gross underestimation of the problem we face.

In history, the process by which things improve has relied not on complacent people who persuade themselves of their own broader perspective and wisdom as they find excuses for doing nothing. Rather, it depends on determined and courageous people who bring about the changes. Cycles occur in history because people make them happen. Nazism came to Germany in the 1930s through deliberate actions, but many people at the time contented themselves with the thought that it couldn't last. They were right only in a strictly limited sense, and wrong about what it would require to reach the point where it ended. It took the extraordinary courage and leadership of people like Winston Churchill and the persistence and sacrifice of millions to turn the cycle—not the complacency of people who sat by and smugly said that this too shall pass.

Higher education became degraded through deliberate action, and it can't be restored to soundness without focused effort. At various points over the past thirty years, many people have thought they were seeing a turn for the better in the universities, and have convinced themselves that academia will naturally heal itself in time. All it usually took was for some noted radical professor to suddenly find that Shakespeare was more than race, gender, and class after all, and wishful thinkers believed they sensed the end of the politically correct campus. But it didn't happen. Roger Kimball noted the pattern more than a decade ago, in 2008: "I have heard several commentators from sundry ideological points of view predict that the reign of political correctness and programmatic leftism on campus had peaked and was about to recede. I wish I could share that optimism. I see no evidence to support it."[16] Events since then have made it abundantly clear that the iron grip of political radicalism on campus grows more absolute with each passing year. It is sheer fantasy to think that it will go away by itself. It won't. It will go away only when the broader society that academia exists to serve (but now doesn't) decides that the destructive rule of radical activists on campus must be brought to an end.

• • •

How exactly can the dismantling of the radical regime be achieved? In practical terms, what can we do? We have one readily available lever of control, and it is a powerful one: the enormous sums of money that we pay for higher education as taxpayers, as parents, and as students. These huge outlays are given with the assumption that they are going to support higher learning, but the reality is that a very large proportion of that money is effectively an involuntary subsidy of radical-left politics. That's clearly not what we all intended, and we have every right to withdraw funding that is so badly misused.

On the campuses, the politicized faculty have an impregnable position; their control is absolute. But they have a crucial weakness in relation to the society they are supposed to serve: they are accepting funds granted with a particular understanding of what they are to be used for, and then diverting them to an unauthorized purpose. That is the very definition of fraud and embezzlement. The public expects students to be taught to think, to analyze, to explore, and to become acquainted with a rich body of historical and theoretical knowledge. The campus is expected to be a place where the political and social issues of the day can be dissected in the careful academic way that is possible only when an issue is looked at from many sides. The present campus regime accepts funding given to it with this understanding and then uses the money instead to promote its destructive radical ideology.

As Kimball aptly puts it, academia "has reneged on its compact with society."[17] In everyday life, when a contract involves payment for a service, and that service is not performed but the money is instead used for the personal purposes of the recipient, further payments can and should be withheld. And so our society has a perfect right to say that it is not getting from academia what it is paying for, and stop the payments. A society that is being defrauded on a grand scale makes itself complicit in the fraud when it knows what is happening and allows it to continue.

Once we recognize that funding diverted to unauthorized uses can and must be terminated, what practical steps can be taken to apply this leverage? There are likely to be a variety of ways it can be done, depending to some extent on particular local conditions and possibilities. If I have convinced the reader that this general direction is the only productive way to proceed, then a range of possible avenues will need to be explored by many shrewd, practical people of good judgment. The following suggestions are only an initial contribution to this exploration.

One obvious place where funding can be reconsidered is in the legislatures that appropriate funds to support state universities. Action by state legislatures will require two things: first, development of the political will to withdraw abused funding as a means of reforming higher education; and second, formulation of an intelligent and workable plan for applying the leverage of withdrawn funding.

As to the first matter—developing the political will for action—we know that the public is aware of the problem in general terms, and that a large segment of the public is already in the mood for serious change. Nevertheless, a campaign to educate the public as to what is happening and why it cannot go on would be extremely useful. One possibility might be a report from a committee of inquiry composed of some distinguished elder statesmen of the *real* academy. A published report could educate parents, students, and voters generally, and make the case for drastic reform. The essence of the case to be made is already clear enough: the nation expends great sums of money so that its children can get an advanced education that will prepare them for careers and citizenship, and those vast sums are being hijacked by political radicals to promote their ideology. Accordingly, higher education must be returned to the control of people who genuinely believe in it. The fact of the misuse of public money by selfish, irresponsible political activists must be at the core of any program of public education.

As to the second issue—deciding on concrete steps through which funding leverage can be made to work—we can expect that all kinds of possible ways of proceeding will be proposed as the idea that drastic reform is essential takes root. A first step is already being taken by the Florida legislature: a report on faculty diversity of opinion has been requested from the state university. The result will surely be so embarrassing that it will automatically lead to some kind of movement for change. It will be interesting to see what the campuses concerned say about their almost total uniformity of opinion.

There is a reform mechanism that is already well known in academia: departments that are judged to be corrupt or dysfunctional are sometimes placed "in receivership." A new department chair is then appointed with independent authority to make new hires in order to bring the department back to health. A legislature might well act similarly by imposing a new management team on a campus, with independent power to make thoroughgoing reforms. That power would have to include the ability to abolish departments 1) whose sole purpose always was political (for example, the notorious "Studies" departments), or 2) that openly proclaim their mission to be political, usually by invoking the need to work for "social justice," or 3) that have become so completely subservient to radical politics that their proper academic mission has now been replaced almost entirely by a political one (as in many sociology, history, and English departments).

One problem that is particularly easy to diagnose is that of political science departments that have completely excluded half the spectrum of political ideas from their faculty roster—a clear sign that a hopelessly radicalized faculty is unable to meet the intellectual standards of a proper university. Depending on the particular circumstances in any given institution, such a condition might require going so far as completely defunding some humanities and social sciences departments, and beginning again from scratch. In these cases, faculty tenure would not necessarily be an obstacle: when an entire department is abolished, the faculty positions it included will no longer exist.

Many variants and combinations of these approaches are possible. A local committee of inquiry might report on changes it finds necessary and then be given the task of implementing them. Or a state legislature might investigate and then cancel funding for departments that are found to be hopelessly corrupted. Serious reform will be a complex matter taking different shapes in different circumstances, but the general aim of reform must always be that those campus units and structures in which excellence in teaching and research has been replaced by fervent radical activism and identity politics must be dismantled, defunded, removed. Only what can coexist with a spirit of free inquiry should be allowed to remain. The diversity bureaucracy should certainly be defunded and dismantled, to end its poisonous influence on the campus.[18] Since the radical left will never cooperate in evaluating the programs and departments that constitute the fiefdoms it has so relentlessly built up over so long a period of time, the essential shape of the situation must be made clear: if there is no fundamental reform of the campus, there will be no money for it.

These are extraordinary measures, and as such they may seem disturbing—but they are far less disturbing than the alternative of letting things go on as they are. What should take our breath away is not how sweeping these reforms would be, but how appalling it is to have a system of higher education that needs them—one so corrupt that it has reduced college education to a travesty of what it once was, and has coarsened and cheapened political debate throughout the nation. That is what should shock us, not how drastic these reform measures are. And let us remember once more: while the case for the actions I've suggested is already powerful, it will be stronger next year, and the year after that, because the absurdity of the campuses will continue to worsen.

Let's return for a moment to those areas of the campuses that are still relatively uncorrupted: much of the STEM fields, and even some small part of the humanities and social sciences. These remaining islands of academic integrity will inevitably deteriorate over time. The base on which reform can build is therefore becoming smaller with every year that passes, which makes reform more and more difficult. Those pockets of quality are assets that we must use while we can, and they give us a powerful reason to act quickly.

Particular reform measures will likely begin on a small scale, in a few states where political opinion is most hospitable. It will certainly be easier for reform to begin in more conservative states, because it's an unfortunate fact that Democrats in state legislatures have seen themselves as protectors of the radicalized campus, as if this were a left-versus-right issue rather than one of the integrity of higher education. But we should recognize that there are actually *three* political groups involved here: traditional liberals as well as conservatives want the first-rate university education for their children that they themselves received, as well as the continuation of the liberal democracy they have always lived in. Neither of those two groups has much in common with faculty radicals, who want something entirely different both for academia and for the nation. Much will depend on whether liberals come to understand that what they really want requires them in this instance to make common cause with conservatives, not with radicals.

If state legislatures recognize a strong bipartisan interest in reforming higher education, they might be motivated to overcome the inertia that protects the status quo. Some states might understand that the situation provides them a great opportunity. Let's suppose that just one state decided to take serious and determined steps to bring its state university back to health and to make it once again a genuine institution of higher learning. Students and faculty from across the nation would flock to that institution. The word would go out: students can get a first-rate education here, and faculty can pursue truth in their fields and debate with their colleagues in a rational way. A state university of that kind would be in a unique position. It would be able to recruit from among all those frustrated scholars working in politicized universities who would be delighted to find a genuine academic workplace again. It might be able to build an outstanding faculty and become the de facto leader of American higher education, whatever the rank it formerly had among the nation's universities. It could become a standard against which all others are compared, because the general public would see a clear example of what it really wants.[19]

Imagine a state somewhere in the heartland of the country whose state university was considered to be in the second tier of major universities: suppose that the state were to realize that it could be the envy of the whole nation by creating a real university again. If its legislature used the power of the purse to compel a return to genuine higher education, its university would quickly acquire an eminence it never had in the past. Given the political will to make a change, that state university could begin a glorious phase in its history. And once this had been done successfully in one state, others would be motivated to do the same. Is the Athens of the next generation somewhere on the Great Plains?

Accreditation agencies might also help reform along, but only if they themselves were first reformed. In recent years they have become obsessed with diversity, which means that to all intents and purposes they have become the enforcers of the politicized campus's agenda—the exact opposite of what they should have been doing. Their original purpose was to guarantee the quality of higher education, but they have allowed themselves to become just one more agent of its corruption. If returned to their proper role, accrediting agencies could be most helpful. For example, they could insist that a political science department with an all-left faculty is incompetent, and withdraw validation of its degree programs. And they could as easily turn their attention to the narrow ideological conformity of almost the entire faculty in the humanities and social sciences, and insist that without a reasonable spectrum of political and social attitudes these sectors of the university too are not competent to give university-level instruction or do university-level research. These judgments are obvious and incontrovertible, and yet accreditation agencies have been hiding from them. If restructured, they might once again pay some attention to academic competence instead of enforcing political correctness.

The federal government's Department of Education could use its influence to steer accreditation agencies back to their proper concern with academic quality. With a change of attitude it should be possible for honest and competent accreditation agencies to help apply the leverage of withdrawn funding. Universities rely on federal funding in all kinds of ways, and those funds now effectively support and encourage a corrupted and politicized higher education. Accreditation agencies could say very simply: If you take federal money that was intended for the support of higher education and use it instead for political reeducation, you'll get no more. Without fundamental reform, there will be no federal money.

Parents are another source of the money that supports our corrupt system of higher education. They too could help to bring about change by declining to pay tuition for radical indoctrination. To a limited extent, they are doing so already: enrollment in higher education has been dropping. In the case of those schools where politically correct lunacy has hit the headlines in recent years, enrollments have plummeted.[20] But that's unfortunately not true across the board in those hundreds of campuses that are just as bad but weren't unlucky enough to attract outside attention.

The natural wish of parents to see their children get qualifications that have always seemed to promise them a better life keeps the campuses afloat in spite of widespread skepticism. But it's likely that parents would seize on better choices once they became aware that particular state universities were making serious systematic reforms. Competition between campuses that in reality are only boot camps for radical political activism and others that have been restored to academic integrity and health would easily be won by the latter. Large numbers of angry and frustrated parents would immediately opt for the real thing.

Yet even in the absence of healthy, unpoliticized campuses, students already have real alternatives. Rather than waste a great deal of money and four years of their lives on learning very little, they can find excellent courses online. If they want to educate themselves in American history—real history, not radical conspiracy-theory fantasy—they can do so with courses of high quality. The same holds for most other fields. A student can now study in his or her own time and pace, getting a genuine education from some of the world's best professors at a tiny fraction of the cost of attending college for four years. It should be possible to organize discussion groups in particular localities to make up for the lack of classroom discussions. If a serious effort were made to acquaint parents with this opportunity for excellent college-level education, free of the foolishness and ideological hatreds of the politicized campuses and at little cost in money and time, large numbers would undoubtedly take it. In doing this, parents would be using the very real leverage available to them to promote college reform, because regular college enrollments would drop sharply.

There are well-known dangers in bringing governmental and public pressures to bear on institutions of higher education, and in normal times we should indeed respect their need for independence, which they usually require if they are to function properly. But when colleges and universities have so willfully ignored the purposes for which their independence was granted, and have corrupted themselves beyond their ability to self-repair, only outside intervention can restore them to the purpose for which they were created. It is certainly predictable that any serious attempt at reform of higher education will be met with howls of outrage from the campus radicals, and those howls will certainly include the cry of "political interference." But such a protest need only be met with derision. Campus radicals complaining about political interference on campus, indeed!

• • •

It was once universally acknowledged that political influence will completely corrupt higher education and make it worthless. We now have before us undeniable proof that it does. We should not have needed to learn so obvious a lesson, but we have, to our very great cost. Another lesson that we have learned, again needlessly, is that identity politics is always an enemy of truth and integrity. Identity politics puts tribal allegiance above considerations of merit and truth; it is incompatible with universities properly understood. Integrity in thought and inquiry always demands that tribalism be set aside.

We should always have understood that when the academic world adopted "diversity" as a core value, it was in effect taking on a political purpose. Had everyone grasped that fact, a loud warning would have sounded: politics was in the process of corrupting academia. Whenever the diversity regime was claimed to be necessary for social justice, the counterargument should have been made: a first-rate educational system in itself does more for social justice and upward mobility than anything else could possibly do. But education can do this only when it stays away from the corrupting effect of direct involvement in political or social causes.

The "Paris Statement" by a group of European scholars (cited in Chapter Four) judged that our universities have been "one of the glories of European civilization." They are that no longer, and our urgent task is to make them so again. Our society can still draw on the trained minds of the citizens who benefited from those institutions when they were indeed glorious, but that won't be possible forever. Vandals are now in control, destroying their glory to remake them for their own selfish purposes. The recent campus riots ought to have convinced any reasonable observer that this problem must be met head-on. The task will be long and difficult: a different campus culture will have to be created. The iron grip of identity politics must be broken, for it cannot coexist with the pursuit of truth.

The measures I've discussed in this chapter will all depend on the public will to reform academia. Ultimately, reform will depend on the people who demand it. It must include an end to the one-party faculty, the removal of radical activists who politicize classrooms, an end to condoning thuggish intolerance, the dismantling of the campus diversity apparatus, the reintroduction of knowledge of and respect for our history and our Constitution, the replacing of cowardly administrators with people who will maintain and protect the integrity of their campuses, and the appointment of trustees who are watchdogs and not lapdogs. In the end, a citizenry that will not accept a thoroughly corrupt higher education must prevail.

ACKNOWLEDGMENTS

My indebtedness to people and institutions who have influenced this book begins with the University of California. My sense of what a great university should be and how it simultaneously advances knowledge and develops its students' ability to think productively owes most to my having been a tenured member of the UC faculty at a time when it was an extraordinary academic enterprise. Participating in UC's faculty self-governance meant working closely with brilliant scholars in all areas of the academy, something far less possible in the British universities where I began my academic career. It was an experience I would not have missed. It was easy then to be proud of the university, and delighted by the company of inspiring faculty colleagues.

A second kind of indebtedness arose in a completely different way: as the process described in the second and third chapters of this book got underway and great institutions of higher learning became increasingly corrupted by radical politics, a quite different source of support and inspiration emerged. Across the country, a relatively small number of courageous, articulate, and resolute individuals began to emerge from the growing majority of academics who were either complicit with what was happening, lazy, or cowardly. They spoke up to proclaim and insist on the real values of the university, and to resist the ongoing corruption of those values. These all too few academic people, though separated geographically, were soon in touch with each other, and came to form a powerful mutually supportive network. I owe more than I can say not just to their analysis and articulation of issues, but to their strength and tenacity, and to their friendship and personal support. To attempt to name them all would run the risk of unjustly omitting some of them. The names of some of them are scattered throughout this book, but one group that I must certainly mention is the board of directors of the California Association of Scholars, of which I have been a member for almost thirty years. They are a remarkable group of brilliant and dedicated academics.

I am indebted also to the authors of the empirical studies on many different issues that I have drawn upon at various points in my narrative. Among these I must single out for special mention the studies of the political affiliations of college faculty by Dan Klein, Mitchell Langbert, and their teams, and the relentless investigations of what is happening on college campuses by David Horowitz.

I am especially indebted to the great skill and care of my copy editor, Carol Staswick. She has improved the manuscript immeasurably. Barbara Ellis, my in-house editor, has been reading and discussing everything I have written for almost half a century; it is hard to imagine what this book or the others I have written would look like without her.

John Ellis
November 2019

NOTES

CHAPTER 1— WHAT DO THOSE NEAR-RIOTS TELL US

1 Stanley Kurtz, "Campus Shout-Down Rate Nearly Quadruples," *National Review*, November 7, 2017.
2 The relevant documents can be found at: Rod Dreher, "The Duke Divinity Crisis: The Documents Are Out," *American Conservative*, May 7, 2017, https://www. theamericanconservative.com/dreher/duke-divinity-crisis-griffiths-documents.
3 Heather Mac Donald, "The Myth of the Racist Cop," *Wall Street Journal*, October 24, 2016.
4 Richard J. Herrnstein and Charles Murray, *The Bell Curve: Intelligence and Class Structure in American Life* (New York: The Free Press, 1994).
5 Richard Sander and Stuart Taylor, Jr., *Mismatch: How Affirmative Action Hurts Students It's Intended to Help, and Why Universities Won't Admit It* (New York: Basic Books, 2012), p. xii.
6 Gail Heriot gives an excellent overview of this controversy, including an analysis of the arguments leveled against Sander, in "Affirmative Action in American Law Schools," San Diego Legal Studies Paper No. 08-041, *Journal of Contemporary Legal Issues*, 17 (2008).
7 Walter E. Williams, "College Destruction of Black Students," *Townhall*, July 4, 2018.
8 Scott Alexander, "Can Things Be Both Popular and Silenced?" Slate Star Codex, May 23, 2018, https://slatestarcodex.com/2018/05/23/can-things-be-both-popular-and-silenced/.

CHAPTER 2—WHO ARE THE PEOPLE DESTROYING OUR UNIVERSITIES?

1 Stanley Rothman, S. Robert Lichter, and Neil Nevitte, "Politics and Professional Advancement Among College Faculty," *The Forum*, 3:1 (2005).
2 Neil Gross and Solon Simmons, "The Social and Political Views of American Professors," September 24, 2007. Though posted on the internet only as a working paper for comment and suggestions, the study was warmly received and provoked much national discussion before the draft was taken down by the authors. It is

available here: https://www.conservativecriminology.com/uploads/5/6/1/7/5617373I/lounsbery_9-25.pdf.

3   Ilya Somin, "Academics' Ideology and 'Moderation,'" *Volokh Conspiracy*, October 9, 2007, http://volokh.com/2007/10/09/academics-ideology-and-moderation.

4   Daniel B. Klein and Andrew Western, "Voter Registration of Berkeley and Stanford Faculty," *Academic Questions*, 18:1 (Winter 2004–5), https://eric.ed.gov/?id=EJ852009.

5   Mitchell Langbert, Anthony J. Quain, and Daniel B. Klein, "Faculty Voter Registration in Economics, History, Journalism, Law, and Psychology," *Econ Journal Watch*, September 2016.

6   Nicholas Quinn Rosenkranz, "Intellectual Diversity in the Legal Academy," *Harvard Journal of Law and Public Policy*, 37:1 (2014), p. 137.

7   Mitchell Langbert, "Homogeneous: The Political Affiliations of Elite Liberal Arts College Faculty," *Academic Questions*, 31:2 (Summer 2018), www.nas.org/articles/homogenous_political_affiliations_of_elite_liberal.

8   Grace Gottschling, "VIDEO: Lawrence Jones talks Kamala Harris, analysis sheds light on potential gold mine," Campus Reform, January 30, 2019, https://www.campusreform.org/?ID=11823.

9   Rosenkranz, "Intellectual Diversity in the Legal Academy," p. 138.

10 James Otteson, "Intellectual Diversity and Academic Professionalism," James R. Martin Center for Academic Renewal, February 21, 2018.

CHAPTER 3—HOW WAS IT POSSIBLE FOR THIS TO HAPPEN?

1   Orrin Hatch, "Identity Politics Threatens the American Experiment," *Wall Street Journal*, May 19, 2018.

2   John Rosenberg aptly describes this progression in the title of an essay: "From Diverse Professors to Professors of Diversity," James G. Martin Center for Academic Renewal, December 7, 2018.

3   Heather Mac Donald, *The Diversity Delusion: How Race and Gender Pandering Corrupt the University and Undermine Our Culture* (New York: St. Martin's Press, 2018).

4   Samuel J. Abrams recently researched the ideology of these "student-facing" campus administrators and found that they are "the most left-leaning group on campus." His general conclusion was that "a *fairly* liberal student body is being taught by a *very* liberal professoriate—and socialized by an *incredibly* liberal group of administrators." I take it that "liberal" here means "left," since most of the people concerned are more radical than liberal. Samuel J. Abrams, "Think Professors Are Liberal? Try School Administrators," Opinion, *New York Times*, October 16, 2018.

5   Christina Hoff Sommers, "Where Title IX Went Wrong," review of *The Transformation of Title IX: Regulating Gender Equality in Education* by R. Shep Melnick, *Education Next*, 19:1 (Winter 2019).

6   George Leef, "Why Can't This Public University Stay Out of Court?" James G. Martin Center for Academic Renewal, April 4, 2018.

7   Philip Hamburger, "Stop Feeding Academic Bloat," *Wall Street Journal*, June 3, 2019.

CHAPTER 4—SABOTAGING EDUCATION FOR CITIZENSHIP

1 Howard Zinn, *A People's History of the United States* (New York: HarperCollins, 1980).
2 Bernard Lewis, "The Roots of Muslim Rage," *Atlantic*, September 1990.
3 "The Paris Statement: A Europe We Can Believe In." This was a manifesto signed in 2017 by a group of scholars from many different European countries: Philippe Bénéton, Rémi Brague, Chantal Delsol, Roman Joch, Lánczi András, Ryszard Legutko, Pierre Manent, Janne Haaland Matlary, Dalmacio Negro Pavón, Roger Scruton, Robert Spaemann, Bart Jan Spruyt, and Matthias Storme.
4 Anne D. Neal and Jerry L. Martin, *Losing America's Memory: Historical Illiteracy in the 21st Century*, American Council of Trustees and Alumni, February 2000, https://www.goacta.org/publications/losing_americas_memory.
5 Even the College Board, which has long had a reputation for objectivity and good sense, has now been politicized: see Stanley Kurtz, "How the College Board Politicized U.S. History," *National Review*, April 25, 2014. For example, the new guidelines for the AP U.S. history exam "will effectively force American high schools to teach U.S. history from a leftist perspective.... The College Board's new and vastly more detailed guidelines can only be interpreted as an attempt to hijack the teaching of U.S. history on behalf of a leftist political and ideological perspective."
6 American Council of Trustees and Alumni, "A Crisis in Civic Education," January 2016, https://www.goacta.org/images/download/A_Crisis_in_Civic_Education.pdf.
7 In South Carolina, college students are required by law to be taught the "essentials of the United States Constitution, the Declaration of Independence, and the Federalist Papers." The relevant law provides that "no student in any such school, college, or university may receive a certificate of graduation without previously passing a satisfactory examination upon the provisions and principles" thereof. But the University of South Carolina's president, Harris Pastides, refuses to comply with that law, on the grounds that it is "archaic." See Hans von Spakovsky's account of this controversy: "University President Calls Law Requiring Study of Constitution 'Archaic,'" *Daily Signal*, July 5, 2014.
8 Heather Mac Donald, *The Diversity Delusion: How Race and Gender Pandering Corrupt the University and Undermine Our Culture* (New York: St. Martin's Press, 2018), p. 213.

CHAPTER 5—GRADUATES WHO KNOW LITTLE AND CAN'T THINK

1 Richard Arum and Josipa Roksa, *Academically Adrift: Limited Learning on College Campuses* (Chicago: University of Chicago Press, 2011).
2 Ibid., pp. 30, 36, 35.
3 The four organizations are: The Conference Board, Corporate Voices for Working Families, Partnership for 21st Century Skills, and the Society for Human Resource Management.
4 This study can be found on the NCES website: National Assessment of Adult Literacy, National Center for Education Statistics, https://nces.ed.gov/naal/kf_dem_edu.asp.

5 Lois Romano, "Literacy of College Graduates Is on Decline: Survey's Finding of a Drop in Reading Proficiency Is Inexplicable, Experts Say," *Washington Post*, December 25, 2005.

6 Arum and Roksa, *Academically Adrift*, p. 56. They are quoting *The American College Teacher: National Norms for 2007–2008*, Higher Education Research Unit, UCLA, 2009.

7 Achieve, Inc., "Rising to the Challenge: Are High School Graduates Prepared for College Work?" February 7, 2005, https://www.achieve.org/publications/rising-challenge-are-high-school-graduates-prepared-college-and-work.

8 Rita Kramer, *Ed School Follies: The Miseducation of America's Teachers* (New York: The Free Press, 1991). Kramer's comments cited in my text are all from her final chapter: "Teaching, Knowledge, and the Public Good."

9 Institute for Higher Education Leadership and Policy, "Consequences of Neglect: Performance Trends in California Higher Education," California State University Sacramento, July 2011.

10 Jay Schalin, "The Politicization of University Schools of Education: The Long March through the Education Schools," James G. Martin Center for Academic Renewal, February 2019.

11 Meghan Grizzle Fischer, Garrett Johnson, and Aaron Ginn, "Viewpoint Diversity in Tech: Reality or Myth?" Lincoln Network, 2018.

12 Eliot Kaufman, "Even the Libertarians Get Lucky Sometimes," *Wall Street Journal*, November 13, 2018.

13 Devorah Goldman, "The Politicization of the MCAT," *Weekly Standard*, April 8, 2018.

14 Stanley Goldfarb, "Take Two Aspirins and Call Me by My Pronouns," *Wall Street Journal*, September 13, 2019. McLean's rebuttal letter was printed in the *Journal* on September 19.

15 Michael J. Pearce, "Politicized Art Schools Are Losing Students to the Atelier Movement," James G. Martin Center for Academic Renewal, May 22, 2019.

16 Walter E. Williams, "Colleges: A Force for Evil," *Jewish World Review*, August 8, 2018.

CHAPTER 6—THE WRETCHED STATE OF THE CAMPUSES

1 James Freeman, "Most U.S. College Students Afraid to Disagree with Professors," *Wall Street Journal*, October 26, 2018.

2 Frank Furedi, "Why More and More Students Won't Speak Up in Class," Minding the Campus, January 8, 2019.

3 Steven F. Rhoads, *Taking Sex Differences Seriously* (San Francisco: Encounter Books, 2004).

4 Higher Education Research Institute, UCLA, "The American College Teacher," Research Brief, March 2009, https://www.heri.ucla.edu/PDFs/pubs/briefs/brief-pr030508-08faculty.pdf. Robin Wilson summarizes the point made here in "Social Change Tops Classic Books in Professors' Teaching Priorities," *Chronicle of Higher Education*, March 5, 2009: "57.8 percent of professors believe it is important to encourage undergraduates to become agents of social change."

5 Robert Edgerton, *Sick Societies: Challenging the Myth of Primitive Harmony* (New York: The Free Press, 1992).

6 Daniel J. McLaughlin, "Young People Feel Politically Empowered, but Politics Doesn't Empower Young People," *Townhall Finance*, June 29, 2018.

7 Documented by Grace Gottschling: "UGA Dean attacked on Twitter for having GOP friend," Campus Reform, July 30, 2018, https://www.campusreform. org/?ID=11170.

8 John Rosenberg, "The University of Virginia in an Uproar Again—Over a Single Faculty Hire," James G. Martin Center for Academic Renewal, August 17, 2018.

9 See Myron Magnet, *The Dream and The Nightmare: The Sixties Legacy to the Underclass* (1993; San Francisco: Encounter Books, 2000), for a horrifying account of the damage that this simplistic approach to political problems can do.

10 Philip S. Babcock and Mindy Marks, "The Falling Time Cost of College: Evidence from Half a Century of Time Use Data," National Bureau of Economic Research Working Paper No. 15954, April 2010.

11 Richard Arum and Josipa Roksa, *Academically Adrift: Limited Learning on College Campuses* (Chicago: University of Chicago Press, 2011), p. 69.

12 Steven Brint, John Aubrey Douglass, Gregg Thompson, and Steve Chatman, *Engaged Learning in a Public University: Trends in the Undergraduate Experience*, Report of the Results of the 2008 University of California Undergraduate Experience Survey, Center for Studies in Higher Education, UC Berkeley, February 2010.

13 Arum and Roksa, *Academically Adrift*, p. 71.

14 Patrick Allitt, "Students Who Don't Study," James G. Martin Center for Academic Renewal, July 28, 2010.

15 UC Santa Cruz Academic Affairs Division, "Tool: Recognizing Microaggressions and the Messages They Send" (Adapted from Derald Wing Sue, *Microaggressions in Everyday Life: Race, Gender and Sexual Orientation*, Wiley & Sons, 2010), https://academicaffairs.ucsc.edu/events/documents/Microaggressions_Examples_ Arial_2014_11_12.pdf.

16 Dennis Prager, "Whatever the Left Touches, It Ruins," *Daily Signal*, April 10, 2018.

17 Dave Rathmanner, "Average Cost of College Statistics for 2019," March 7, 2018, LendEDU, https://lendedu.com/blog/average-cost-of-college-statistics.

CHAPTER 7—THE CAMPUS WORLD OF LIES AND DECEIT

1 Christina Hoff Sommers, *Who Stole Feminism? How Women Have Betrayed Women* (New York: Simon & Schuster, 1994).

2 Heather Mac Donald, *The Diversity Delusion: How Race and Gender Pandering Corrupt the University and Undermine Our Culture* (New York: St. Martin's Press, 2018), chap. 6, "The Campus Rape Myth."

3 Ibid., pp. 121–22.

4 Ibid., p. 123.

5 Jarrett Stepman, "Fabricating Hate Crimes Is a Byproduct of Victim Ideology on Campus," *Daily Signal*, October 18, 2018.

6 Eddie Scarry, "November 2018 was college hate crime hoax month," *Washington Examiner*, December 3, 2018.

7 Judith Butler, "Further Reflections on the Conversations of Our Time," *Diacritics*, 27 (1997).

8 The definitive account of the hoax and its aftermath is *The Sokal Hoax: The Sham That Shook the Academy*, ed. by the editors of *Lingua Franca* (Lincoln: University of Nebraska Press, 1996).

9 For an overview of the activities of the three authors, see Jillian Kay Melchior, "Fake News Comes to Academia," *Wall Street Journal*, October 6–7, 2018.

10 Phillip W. Magness, "What the Hoax Papers Tell Us about the Decline of Academic Standards," James G. Martin Center for Academic Renewal, November 28, 2018.

11 American Academy of Arts and Sciences, "Bachelor's Degrees in the Humanities," Humanities Indicators, updated May 2017, https://www.humanitiesindicators.org/content/indicatordoc.aspx?i=34.

12 Benjamin Schmidt, "The Humanities Are in Crisis," *Atlantic*, August 23, 2018.

13 Tim Ciccotta, "University of Wisconsin Campus Considers Eliminating 13 Majors, Including English, History, Philosophy," *Breitbart*, March 22, 2018.

14 Roger Kimball, *Tenured Radicals*, 3rd ed. (Chicago: Ivan R. Dee, 2008), p. xxxviii.

15 California Association of Scholars, *A Crisis of Competence: The Corrupting Effect of Political Activism in the University of California*, A Report Prepared for the Regents of the University of California, April 2012, https://nas.org/storage/app/media/Reports/A%20Crisis%20of%20Competence/A_Crisis_of_Competence.pdf.

CHAPTER 8—WHAT CAN BE DONE TO RESTORE HIGHER EDUCATION?

1 Kevin Jackson's apt phrase, from *The Kevin Jackson Radio Show*.

2 UC Santa Cruz, Academic Personnel, Applicant Diversity Statements, https://apo.ucsc.edu/employment/applicant-diversity-statements.html.

3 UC Santa Cruz, Open Recruitments, Physical and Biological Sciences: Biomedical Sciences – Assistant Professors (Initial Review 11/08/19), https://recruit.ucsc.edu/JPF00756; Computer Science and Engineering: Assistant Professor in Deep Learning (Initial Review 1/07/20), https://recruit.ucsc.edu/JPF00769.

4 Two members of the Villanova University faculty wrote in opposition to the new diversity questions in teaching evaluations: Colleen A. Sheehan and James Matthew Wilson, "A Mole Hunt for Diversity 'Bias' at Villanova," *Wall Street Journal*, March 29, 2019. Sheehan and Wilson were instantly denounced in a letter signed by over a hundred of their colleagues. Discussion of the pros and cons of such policy questions is no longer to be allowed.

5 Heather Mac Donald, *The Diversity Delusion: How Race and Gender Pandering Corrupt the University and Undermine Our Culture* (New York: St. Martin's Press, 2018), p. 193.

6 Ben Cohen shows how campus radicals are now targeting the field of engineering and attempting to impose on it their social justice goals, e.g. to "bar engineers from designing prisons, working on defense projects, or working in formerly state-run industries." Cohen, "The Rise of Engineering's Social Justice Warriors," James G. Martin Center for Academic Renewal, November 21, 2018.

7 David Randall and Christopher Welser, *The Irreproducibility Crisis in Modern Science: Causes, Consequences, and the Road to Reform*, National Association of Scholars, April 2018, https://www.nas.org/images/documents/NAS_irreproducibilityReport.pdf.

8 Paul Jump, "Slay peer review 'sacred cow', says former BMJ chief," *Times Higher Education (THE)*, April 21, 2015.

9 An excellent brief account of the Enstrom episode is by Jerome C. Arnett, Jr., in "Politicized Science: The Case of Dr. James Enstrom v. Powerful Environmental Activists," *Journal of American Physicians and Surgeons*, 17:4 (Winter 2012).

10 See for example: George Leef, "Stanley Kurtz on North Carolina's Campus Free-Speech Act," *National Review*, May 29, 2018. Another example is an essay by Joyce Lee Malcolm, "Building a Culture of Free Expression on the American College Campus," American Council of Trustees and Alumni, April 2018, https://www.goacta.org/publications/building-a-culture-of-free-expression-on-the-american-college-campus. These are both fine essays in many ways, but they do not offer real solutions to the problem that we are facing.

11 Report of the Committee on Freedom of Expression, University of Chicago, https://provost.uchicago.edu/sites/default/files/documents/reports/FOECommitteeReport.pdf.

12 David Horowitz chronicled his attempts to promote his Academic Bill of Rights in two books: *Indoctrination U: The Left's War Against Academic Freedom* (New York: Encounter Books, 2007), and *Reforming Our Universities: The Campaign for an Academic Bill of Rights* (Washington, D.C.: Regnery, 2010).

13 Jonathan Haidt and Greg Lukianoff, "The Coddling of the American Mind," *Atlantic*, September 2015. This article was later expanded into a book with the same title, published by Penguin Books in 2018.

14 Daniel J. McLaughlin, "Young People Feel Politically Empowered, but Politics Doesn't Empower Young People," *Townhall Finance*, June 29, 2018.

15 For example: *Against Deconstruction* (Princeton: Princeton University Press, 1989), and *Literature Lost: Social Agendas and the Corruption of the Humanities* (New Haven & London: Yale University Press, 1997).

16 Roger Kimball, *Tenured Radicals*, 3rd ed. (Chicago: Ivan R. Dee, 2008), p. xlii.

17 Ibid., p. xxxvi.

18 Abolishing the diversity bureaucracy is suggested by Heather Mac Donald in *The Diversity Delusion*, p. 186.

19 Warren Treadgold, in *The University We Need: Reforming American Higher Education* (New York: Encounter Books, 2018), suggests another way of creating a model university, one that would need wealthy philanthropists to make a gift large enough to start a new university from scratch. This new institution would also recruit from the genuine academics remaining in American higher education. If this were to happen, the new campus thus created would certainly be oversubscribed, resulting in a demand for more of the like. Whether a gift in the amount needed could be found is uncertain, but the idea of creating competition for the politicized campuses goes in the right direction.

20 A partial boycott by students and parents has already been seen in the case of the University of Missouri, where public knowledge of a particularly foolish piece of politically correct nonsense in the autumn of 2015 caused a serious decline in enrollments. According to a report in 2017, "Freshman enrollment at the Columbia campus, the system's flagship, has fallen by more than 35 percent in the two years since. The university administration acknowledges that the main reason is a backlash from the events of 2015, as the campus has been shunned by students and families." Anemona Hartocollis, "Long After Protests, Students Shun the University of Missouri," *New York Times*, July 9, 2017.

INDEX